[uhg-lee] /'ʌg li/

ug·ly

resumes
get
JOBS!

...and other FISHING lessons

JENNIFER RALLIS | THEO RALLIS

©2009 NMGN Publishing | Second Edition 2009

All rights reserved

Printed in the United States of America

No part of this book may be reproduced, stored in a retrieval system, or transmitted, in any form or by any means, electronic, mechanical, photocopying, recording, or otherwise without the prior written permission of the copyright holder.

For permission to use material from this guide, contact us at www.uglyresumes.com.

Every effort has been made to trace ownership of all copyrighted material and to secure permission from copyright holders.

Publisher's Note

The scanning, uploading, and distribution of this book via the Internet or via other means without the permission of the publisher is illegal and punishable under the law. Please purchased only authorized electronic editions, and do not participate in or encourage electronic piracy of copyrighted materials. Your support of the author's rights is appreciated.

Books are available at quantity discounts, contact sales@uglyresumes.com.

Limit of Liability/Disclaimer of Warranty: While the publisher and authors have used their best efforts in preparing this book, they make no representation or warranties with respect to the accuracy or completeness of the contents of this book and specifically disclaim any implied warranties of merchantability or fitness for a particular purpose. The advice and strategies contained herein may not be suitable for your situation. Neither the publisher nor author shall be liable for any loss of profit or any other damages, including but not limited to special, incidental, consequential, or other damages.

ISBN is   0-615-30964X   EAN-13 is 978-0-615-30964-4

To order your copy, visit
www.uglyresumes.com

For corporate or volume orders, contact
sales@uglyresumes.com

[uhg-lee] /ˈʌg li/

ug·ly

resumes
get
JOBS!

This book is dedicated to our little ones.

The Inspiration

This book was inspired by an exceptional candidate who emailed me his resume on a very hectic day. This candidate had a remarkable record of employment, extraordinary technical skills and a first-rate education. Despite his outstanding qualifications and my greatest intentions, I never spoke with him and his application never progressed any further.

What was the stumbling block? Our state-of-the-art applicant tracking system (a software application we used to manage candidates, clients and job openings) was unable to read the elaborate design of his resume. As a result, his resume was filed away in our "Candidates to Enter" folder where it joined 563 other resumes!

In spite of our best efforts, weeks later his resume still sat in the "Candidates to Enter" folder, and I found myself thinking about this gentleman. How many other companies had he applied to? How many times had his resume disappeared in the process? Without follow-up, he was unaware of the plight of his application. If this could happen at our small recruiting firm, then how often was it happening at larger companies? And how many candidates was this happening to? The big black hole of resumes did exist!

With these thoughts and the words of encouragement from a friend, I scripted a cheat sheet of sorts for job seekers on creating a technology friendly resume. I wanted to share insider secrets on avoiding the big black hole of resumes and how a job seeker can increase the number of recruiters who view their resume in a database of millions of candidates. Within a few weeks, my cheat sheet was done and the Ugly Resume was born! I knew, however, that a great resume wasn't enough to get a job in today's highly competitive and exceedingly technical employment market. A successful candidate would need more.

Then as fate would have it, my husband Theo (a process consultant) was tossed back into the job market to compete with hundreds of thousands of other job seekers. You would think having a wife as a recruiter would have been a good thing, but with no available job openings then it's moot. In a last ditched effort to be of some help, I handed Theo my Ugly Resume guide. At that point, it consisted of handwritten lists of job boards and barely legible pages of job hunting tips I had collected over the years, all compiled in a well worn notebook. Along with it I added a warning that in this slowing economy his job search was going to take months longer than he ever anticipated!

Within a couple of weeks to my surprise he had spoken to several hiring managers and had more than a few interviews lined up! A couple of weeks later, he was in the running for four different jobs and two of which weren't even in his industry! Amazed at his results, I asked how he did it. He explained that he had gone to the bookstore hoping he could locate a step-by-step guide on how to find a job. All he found were books with irrelevant sample resumes and lists upon lists of outdated job boards. Frustrated with his trip to the bookstore, he painstakingly read through my disorganized collection of notes and found the makings of a job search system. With a little added research, he put it together in an easy to follow process and had found great success in a downturned economy. This process was the missing piece job seekers needed!

In the weeks following, Theo abandoned his own job search and we focused on creating the ultimate job search system – **Ugly Resumes Get Jobs – And Other Fishing Lessons**. *We wanted to share this with job seekers and give them the upper hand in today's highly competitive job market. It is our sincere wish that* **Ugly Resumes Get Jobs** *helps you find fulfillment in your next great job.*

Jennifer Rallis 2009

Table of Contents

TEACH A MAN TO FISH 1

CHOOSE A FISHING SPOT 7

1. Focus your job search 8
2. Dealing with The emotional side of your job search 10
3. Rules of the search 12

GET YOUR TACKLE BOX READY 19

1. The ugly resume – the basics 20
2. Create the ugly resume 25
3. Create a basic introduction email 39

DON'T FORGET YOUR FISHING POLE 49

1. Build your brand 50

LET'S GO FISHING 61

1. Job search etiquette 62
2. Where recruiters advertise jobs 63
3. How online job boards work 71
4. Dispelling the myths about how companies recruit & how to overcome them 76

FINDING SECRET FISHING HOLES 87

1. Proactive job search strategies 88
2. Passive job search strategies 94
3. Connect with key decision makers 97

LAND YOUR TROPHY FISH 105

1. What recruiters look for 106
2. Ace the interview – do's and don'ts 107
3. Follow up 113
4. How much are you worth? 115
5. Offer negotiations 116
6. How to accept/decline offers 118

PLAN THE FISHING TRIP 121

1.   Using the success map 122

CASE STUDIES 131

1.   Case study i – Jack Wiseman 132
2.   Case study ii – Susan McMaster 141

YOUR PROFILE 149

KEYWORDS 159

JOB BOARDS 165

Give a man a fish and you have fed him for a day. Teach a man to fish and you have fed him for a lifetime.

Unknown

Give a man the help wanted ads and you have kept him busy for a day. Teach a man to find a job and you have freed him for a lifetime.

Theo and Jen Rallis 2009

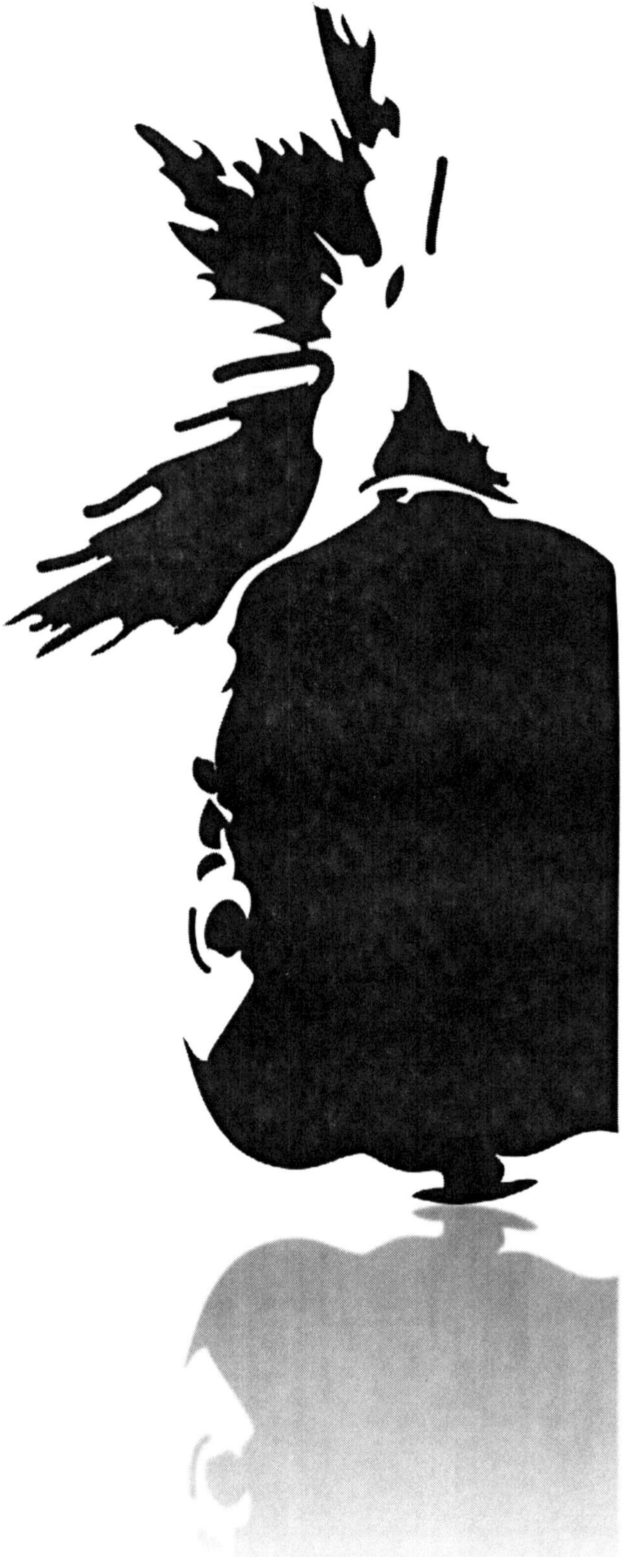

TEACH A MAN TO FISH

CHAPTER 00

Aimlessly surfing the web, randomly applying to hundreds of jobs is the perfect recipe for exhaustion, frustration, anger and defeat. No more! Redefine your job search and regain control of your future today.

RIGHT-SIZED, DOWN-SIZED OR JUST AGONIZED?

You have found help with Ugly Resumes Get Jobs and Other Fishing Lessons. In the upcoming chapters we are going to teach you how to find a great job in today's highly competitive, dreadfully complicated and exceedingly technical employment market.

Ugly Resumes Get Jobs and Other Fishing Lessons is a powerful job search tool consisting of:

- a) the system and tools provided here, and
- b) support through our online community (*www.uglyresumes.com*)

HOW TO USE THE BOOK

This is a not a book to be read, rather a process to be followed.

The book is divided into seven chapters and four appendixes. For the book to be effective, you must:

1) read the chapters in order (*do not skip ahead*)
2) complete all assigned tasks at the end of each chapter
3) use your *Success Map*

Your job search will begin with the important tasks of: defining your job search goal, creating an effective, technology friendly resume, branding and planning. By the end of Chapter Seven, you will begin your job search using the *Success Map*.

As you embark on your search for new employment, you will soon discover that each company has its own unique system to recruit new employees. Some companies use state-of-the-art technology and employ specialized recruiters whose job is to locate, evaluate and secure new employees for their organizations. While other companies lack technology and rely on personal referrals (the good ole' boy network) to find new employees for their businesses. And still other companies outsource their entire recruitment process to third party recruiters. To further complicate matters, each company will have a unique method of interviewing, conducting reference checks and negotiating salary.

Knowing that each company is unique, we have put together a general job search strategy that will help you navigate today's employment market. To simplify things, we use the general term "recruiter" to refer to anyone who is involved in the hiring process.

As a bonus, we have included important *tips and techniques* throughout the book using the following characters:

DO this!

FISHING LESSON: Important information that will help your job search

DON'T do this!

WARNING: This book is intended for job seekers who are able to navigate the Internet. If you do not understand how to use the Internet, we suggest visiting your local library or government employment office for a training class.

Focus your job search	8
The emotional side of job hunting	10
Rules of the search	12

CHOOSE A FISHING SPOT

CHAPTER 01

To catch a trophy fish you must choose your fishing spot wisely and have the emotional stamina to keep tossing your line into the water, even when you doubt a fish will ever bite.

In this chapter we will help you define your job search goal and help you develop the emotional stamina necessary for a successful job search.

1. FOCUS YOUR JOB SEARCH

The first step in a successful job search is defining your goal. To begin, you must answer a very important question:

What type of job do I want?

Don't answer right away. You owe it to yourself to take some time and think about your answer. Whether you have been tossed into the job market by an unforeseen downsizing or have chosen to search for new employment, you have been given an opportunity to reevaluate your career. Don't waste it!

Don't dismiss the importance of this exercise. Without focus and a clear mind you will squander precious time.

Our point is *not* to convince you to give up the career you have worked so hard for to pursue a grand dream of becoming *CEO of Consumer Product for GE.* Most of you will be very happy with your chosen career; however, if you have been suffering for months and know that there is something else you would like to do, then this is the time for change.

Before moving forward, you must have a clear picture of the type of job you want. This picture is crucial for a successful job search. If you cannot clearly define what you want, we **can't** help you find it.

Some of the questions you need to ask yourself are:

How much money do I want to earn? Will the career I have chosen earn me that income?

What did I like most about my previous jobs?

If I could do anything what would it be?

What sort of job responsibilities do I want?

Is position and status important to me?

Where do I want to work? Is this an opportunity for relocation?

Do I enjoy traveling for work?

How much time do I want to spend commuting?

What type of company do I want to work for? (Fortune 500, family owned or environmentally conscious)

Is this where I envisioned I would be 10 years ago? And where do I want to be 5, 10, 20 years from now?

Am I willing to take a risk and start down a new career path?

2. DEALING WITH THE EMOTIONAL SIDE OF YOUR JOB SEARCH

Searching for a new job is without a doubt, stressful! It has been documented by numerous mental health organizations to be one of life's most stressful events.

The stress associated with losing one job and finding another isn't surprising when you consider the basic employee - employer relationship. Employers hire employees to fulfill a business need. As long as the business need exists and the employee is profitable, he will continue to have a job. An employee accepts employment to earn money to maintain a suitable lifestyle. As the relationship develops, the employer remains focused on the bottom line. The employee; however, begins to focus less on the monetary aspects of the job and more on the intangibles of the position. The employee develops social networks with coworkers and an identity associated with his job title, responsibilities and being part of the company. Most employees derive a sense of self worth and purpose from their job and being able to provide a steady paycheck to support their families.

When the employer - employee relationship is disrupted either by an unfavorable change in work conditions or an unforeseen downsizing, the effects on the employee can be devastating. Not only may an employee be left wondering how he will pay his monthly bills, but loss of self-worth and feelings of isolation and rejection may consume the employee as the intangibles of his job disappear. If you have these feelings, you are not alone. Take a deep breath we are going to help you.

To endure your job search you must develop the emotional stamina to keep going even when you feel that you have exhausted every possible lead. The reality is that you haven't exhausted every possibility until you have found your next great job!

To maintain your sanity, you must live by the following rules outlined in the next section.

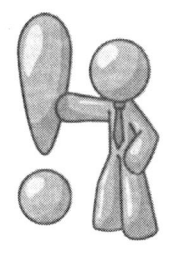

To cope with the stress of unemployment take some action every day. Send an email to a hiring manager or apply for a job online, it will ease your mind that you have taken some action.

3. RULES OF THE SEARCH

Earmark this page and refer to it often.

Reduce financial stressors in your life:

If you are unemployed, budget your money. Choose home-brewed coffee in the morning versus your $5 gourmet coffee at the local café; renovations, vacations and eating out need to be put on the back burner. Speak to your bank and credit card companies; in some circumstances these institutions will give you payment extension periods. Don't wait, start your budget immediately after losing your job. Savings can quickly dwindle and your job search may take months longer than you anticipate.

Only your mom will feel sorry for you:

Regardless of why you lost your job or why you want to leave your current one, you need to surround yourself with positive people. Venting is not a constructive act, but taking action is. Ensure that those in your inner circle are feeding your fire for change.

Carpe Diem:

Take a few minutes every day and enjoy this new found freedom. When was the last time you didn't have to think about your boss, customers or the *TPS Reports* that were due every Monday? Your Blackberry is quiet…that's a good thing!

Consider your job search a full-time job:

Set aside 5-7 hours a day for job searching. Do not spend your day aimlessly surfing the internet or running errands. You don't have time to squander, you will work harder at this than you ever imagined! Wake up early every morning, get dressed, and follow your *Success Map*.

Accept the reality:

Accept that your job search will take much longer than you ever anticipated. Job seekers often underestimate the time it will take to find a job and are left with feelings of failure and disappointment when they don't find employment right away.

Avoid failure:

Don't set yourself up for failure by applying to jobs that you are either over-qualified or under-qualified for. Don't assume that because you hold a PhD in Physics, the local burger joint will

This too shall pass. Do not focus on what you've lost or the horrible job you have, focus on what will be gained.

be honored that you have applied for a job and hire you on the spot!

Don't take it personally:

Don't take a company's decision to decline your application personal. Companies hire based on business needs not personal needs. Accept their decision and move on; a better job awaits you!

Accept the stress:

Stress is a normal part of everyone's job search. You will have wonderful days and stress-filled days. Exercise is a great way to relieve stress, do something physical every day.

Evaluate your progress:

Each week evaluate your weekly progress. Look at what is working for you and what isn't. Do more of the things that are working for you. And develop new approaches for the things that are not working. For example, if certain job boards are producing better results then use them more often. If hiring managers are not returning your calls, then tweak your mini-commercial (see Chapter Two).

Reward yourself:

Don't let your job search consume you. Take some time each day to go for a walk, clean the garage, or have a coffee with a friend.

TASKS:

Now that you have read Chapter One, it is time to define your job search goal. What type of job do you want? Don't assume you already know the answer! You owe it to yourself to take some time and consider your answers carefully.

1. Answer the following questions in the space provided:

    How much money would I like to earn?

    Will the career I have chosen earn me that income?

    What did I like most about my previous jobs?

    If I could do anything what would it be?

    What sort of job responsibilities do I want?

    Is position and status important to me?

    Where do I want to work? Is this an opportunity for relocation?

    Do I enjoy traveling for work?
    How much time do I want to spend commuting?

In the beginning the benefits of the exercises found at the end of the chapters may seem unfruitful, but through determined effort comes monumental results.

What type of company do I want to work for? (Fortune 500, family owned or environmentally conscious)

Is this where I envisioned I would be 10 years ago?

Where would I like to be 5, 10, 20 years from now?

Am I willing to take a risk and start down a new career path?

2. Now that you have a clearer picture of what you want, complete the following sentence,

   I am looking for a _____ job. In this role, I will likely have the following title _____

3. Earmark *Rules of Search*

4. Reduce your stress, spend ½ hour doing something physical.

THE UGLY RESUME – THE BASICS	20
CREATING THE UGLY RESUME	25
CREATING A BASIC INTRODUCTION EMAIL	39

GET YOUR TACKLE BOX READY

CHAPTER 02

If you want to land a trophy fish, you must load your tackle box with the right fishing gear. Landing your next great job is no different. In this chapter we will arm you with the necessary tools for a successful job search. We will:

Create an Ugly Resume specifically designed for today's technology driven employment market.

Create an introduction email that will entice recruiters to call you!

1. THE UGLY RESUME – THE BASICS

In the past fifteen years, technology has significantly changed how companies attract job seekers, screen potential candidates and manage the hiring process. In today's technology driven job market, companies use the Internet to attract job seekers; use automated online questionnaires to screen potential candidates and leverage software packages called *applicant tracking systems* (ATS) to manage their hiring process. As companies have embraced technology and moved forward with leaps and bounds, a large number of job seekers still use antiquated resume styles that predate the Internet! The job market has changed and so must your resume!

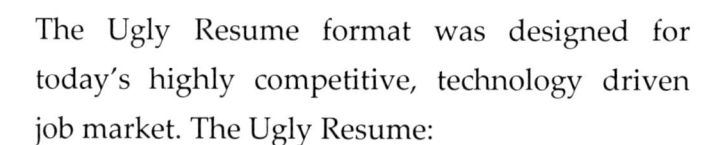

Ugly Resumes Get Jobs!

The Ugly Resume format was designed for today's highly competitive, technology driven job market. The Ugly Resume:

- *Paints a picture of a successful person companies will line up to hire*
- *Is easily downloaded into most online job tracking systems -avoiding the infamous black hole of resumes*

- *Increases the number of recruiters who view the resume by increasing the database search ranking*

The Ugly Resume is the result of years of reviewing hundreds of thousands of resumes, understanding what works and what doesn't, working and speaking with hiring authorities about how they screen resumes and having performed a thorough evaluation of the recruiting technologies commonly used in today's job market.

Before we discuss the specifics section of the Ugly Resume, there are six general rules that need to be reviewed:

In today's technology driven employment market the content and file type of your resume is by far more important than the appearance of the resume.

i] CREATE TWO UGLY RESUMES, A .DOC FILE AND A .TXT (PLAIN TEXT) FILE

Today it isn't the *pretty* resumes that get jobs, it is the *Ugly*! The Ugly Resume will challenge you to rethink resume writing. Traditional *pretty* resumes with elaborate fonts, graphics, headers, footers and text boxes are intended to look good - not to be successfully downloaded into a database. Depending on the technology used by a hiring company, simple things like text boxes may prevent your resume from downloading

Planning to take and have taken are two different things.

Don't include skills and education that you do NOT have on your resume!

properly and leave you stranded in the infamous black hole! Although nothing can guarantee a proper download, using the Ugly Resume format will significantly increase the chances that your resume is captured and processed correctly.

Two formats of the Ugly Resume are required. A WORD (.doc) version is used when the resume is sent as an attachment in an email or is printed off for a personal interview. The plain.txt version is used to apply online at a company's career site or to submit to an online job board.

ii]   USE KEYWORDS

Using plenty of keywords (specific to your industry) is the most effective way to increase the number of recruiters who view your resume in a database of potentially millions of other job seekers. These keywords may include specific software, training, designations or accreditations, job titles, post-secondary schools, names of previous employers, etc. Recruiters will often conduct database searches on these terms, be sure to include both the abbreviation and the full term.

iii] KEEP THE FORMAT SIMPLE

Do not include fancy fonts, text boxes or graphics. Although your resume may look appealing, these things may prevent your resume from properly downloading into a company's career site or an online job board. An improperly downloaded resume may not appear when a recruiter conducts a database search or may lack important details, such as your contact information.

iv] WRITE THE RESUME IN THIRD PERSON OBJECTIVE

Do not write the resume in the first person using "I". For example, *I managed a team of 8 Customer Service Representatives* should read, *Managed a team of 8 Customer Service Representatives.*

v] ENSURE THERE ARE NO SPELLING OR GRAMMATICAL ERRORS IN THE RESUME

We know hiring managers who immediately discard resumes with spelling errors.

Have a friend carefully review your resume, checking for spelling errors, missing words, etc - before you send it out to potential employers.

vi] DO NOT INCLUDE AN OBJECTIVE

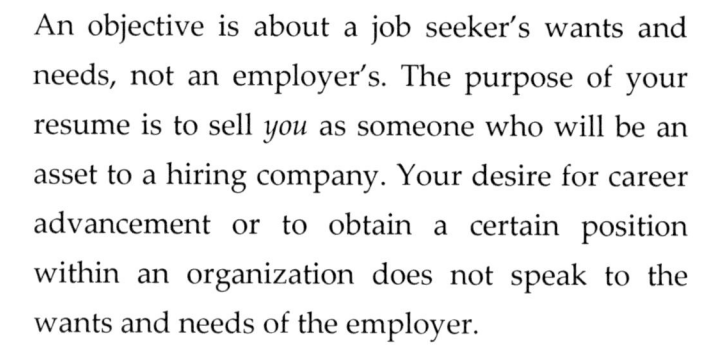

An objective is about a job seeker's wants and needs, not an employer's. The purpose of your resume is to sell *you* as someone who will be an asset to a hiring company. Your desire for career advancement or to obtain a certain position within an organization does not speak to the wants and needs of the employer.

Imagine receiving a solicitation letter from a major credit card company *Objective: To entice you to use this card and charge you thousands of dollars in tremendously high interest rates and usage fees making us very rich.*

Instead credit card companies speak to *your* wants and needs, offering you the freedom to buy whatever you want, take a much needed vacation or pay off other credit card debt.

Like these companies you must speak to the wants and needs of your customer, the employer.

Don't use spreadsheet programs, such as Microsoft Excel, to create your resume. Only use word processing programs such as Microsoft Word.

2. CREATE THE UGLY RESUME

The Ugly Resume consists of the following nine sections:

- *Contact Information*
- *Profile*
- *Education*
- *Licenses and Certifications*
- *Additional Training*
- *Technical Skills*
- *Employment History*
- *References*
- *Citizenship Status*

Each of these sections are detailed in the following pages. At the end of the chapter, we will help you create your own Ugly Resume. *Refer to Appendix-A to see sample Ugly Resumes or visit* www.uglyresumes.com.

i] CONTACT INFORMATION

Make the process of contacting you easy for a recruiter. In this section provide plenty of accurate contact information. Include the following:

First and Last Name

Day Time Phone Number(s)

Email Address

Optional: Mailing Address

First and Last Name

Include both your first and last name at the top of the resume. If you are known by a nick name that is different than your legal name, include that name on your resume. For example, *Constantine Angelopoulos* would record *Gus Angelopoulos* at the top of his resume. This will lessen any confusion surrounding your application, especially when the hiring company conducts reference checks.

Note: *Hyphenated last names confuse most software programs. As an example, Helen Ottewell-McCartney may download as: Helen Ottewell-McCartney or Helen Ottewell or Ottewell McCartney*

Be sure to update all potential employers with any changes to your telephone number or email address.

or Helen McCartney. With all these variations it may be difficult for a recruiter to locate her in a database. To lessen any confusion surrounding your application, we suggest recording only your second last name on your resume. In the above example, the candidate would record her name as Helen McCartney.

When you are hired by a company, then provide your full name as it appears on your legal documents.

Daytime Phone Number

Most recruiters will contact you during regular business hours. It is important that you make yourself available by providing a daytime phone number such as a cell number. If you are unable to speak freely at work, do not include your work number on your resume!

Email Address

Email has quickly become the normal method of communication in the business world. Online applications will require an email address and many recruiters will use email as their primary method of communication. It is important to include a valid email address on your resume, but there are some rules to consider regarding your email address:

- Do not include a current work email address. Work email is the property of your employer. Under the law in most jurisdictions, employers have the right to monitor (*read*) employee email.

- Carefully choose your email address. A poorly chosen email address is bad branding and may prevent your application from moving forward. For example:

  o Always_late_4_work@freemail.com or FiredAgain@freemail.com or Lazy_Boy@freemail.com

  o Absolutely **DO NOT** use sexual language or profanity in your email address!

The following sites offer free email service:

www.hotmail.com, www.gmail.com and www.yahoo .com.

Signing up for an account takes only a few minutes and you will be able to access your email anywhere in the world!

Mailing Address

A mailing address is optional on your resume. Due to privacy issues, many candidates chose not to include a mailing address.

Warning: *If you are trying to relocate from another country, do not disguise this fact by omitting your address. As work visas are involved in these situations, a recruiter may feel that you were deliberately deceptive by omitting your address.*

A FINAL NOTE REGARDING CONTACT INFORMATION:

Do not include the following information:

- **Personal Websites:**

    A resume is a business document intended for a business audience; do not include personal websites in your contact information. Innocent information found on your personal website may send the wrong message to a potential employer and prevent your application from moving forward.

    For example: A personal website depicting a dedicated father who coaches his son's baseball team and his daughter's soccer team and enjoys spending lots of time with his children, applying for a job that requires 85% travel and long work hours.

- **Photos:**

    Do not include a personal photo on your resume.

If you author a business related blog that showcases your industry expertise, then include it in your contact information.

ii] PROFILE

Third party recruiters and professional resume writing specialists know that the secret to getting a resume noticed is to create a mini commercial (*a profile*) at the beginning of the resume. The profile consists of eight to twelve points which highlight a job seeker's key accomplishments and details why that person is a *perfect fit* for a specific position or company. Unlike the rest of the Ugly Resume, the profile is customized for each specific position applied to.

When writing your profile, do not assume that the person reading your resume can see that you are the *best* person for the job - you must spell it out to them! To learn how to create an effective profile, please refer to *Appendix B*.

iii] EDUCATION

In this section include all degrees and diplomas you have completed. As recruiters often conduct database searches for specific degrees or schools, it is important to include as much information about your post-secondary education as possible. List your degrees in order of completion, most recent degree first.

Be sure you have original copies of your diplomas, degrees and certificates. Potential employers may request to see them.

Include:

- Full Name of School
- Campus Attended (City, State and if outside of North America, include the Country)
- Full Name of Degree
- Major Area of Study
- Optional: Year Graduated and/or GPA

Example:

1990   University of Guelph, Guelph, ON
Bachelor of Applied Science – Major Psychology

Do not include partial (*incomplete*) degrees unless you are currently enrolled in a program and have a scheduled graduation date within the next four years. Listing incomplete degrees shows that you are person who doesn't finish things. **Some things are left best unsaid.**

Hint: *If you lack a post-secondary diploma or degree, do not include an education section on your resume. Including your high school diploma draws needless attention to the fact that you have not completed additional education.* **The exception** – *if the job*

If you have all the required experience listed in a job posting, but lack the "preferred education", apply to the job anyway. Some companies value experience over education!

posting requires a high school diploma, then include it!

Hint: *Do not include "Life Experience" degrees. There are several websites posing as legitimate post-secondary institutions. For a fee these "schools" translate employment history and life experience into a suitable bachelors. Many employers do not consider these legitimate and will discard resumes that include these degrees.*

iv] LICENSES AND CERTIFICATIONS

In this section list all licenses and certifications you have completed, recruiters will often conduct database searches on these credentials. Include the full name of the certification/license, as well as the abbreviation and the year the license or certification was earned.

For example: Microsoft Certified Solution Developer (MCSD) 2008

v] TECHNICAL SKILLS

Don't miss an opportunity to be found! Recruiters will often conduct database searches on specific technical skills. In this section list all the software, hardware and/or systems skills you possess. Do not over embellish your skill set. At

Don't list obsolete software and hardware on your resume. These antiquated skills will depict you as someone who is behind-the-times.

some point you may be called to task and if it is discovered that you have lied, your application may be immediately discarded. Be sure to include software versions.

vi] ADDITIONAL TRAINING

In this section include all professional training you have completed. Detail the year you took the course (*optional*), the name of the course and who offered the training. For example:

2003   How to Sell Over the Phone
         Telemarketing Institute of Miami

vii] EMPLOYMENT HISTORY

Employment history is typically the largest section of the resume. In this section, you will need to include enough information about your previous employment to provide a clear picture of your experience, but don't overwhelm the reader with too many details. Include the following information in the Employment History section:

Dates of Employment

Company Name

Company Location

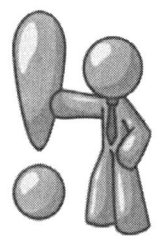

If you worked for a temporary agency or contract house on site at another business, list the agency / contract house as your employer and add "onsite at (include of name of customer)"

Company Website Address

Title

Functional Title

Job Responsibilities

Reason for Leaving (Optional)

Dates of Employment

It is important to include your dates of employment with each employer. From a recruiter's view point, it looks suspicious when no dates of employment are included or the vague 2004- 2008 standard is used on a resume. Include your start month and year and end month and year (or till *Pres*). As most companies conduct standard verification of employment as part of their screening process, ensure that these dates are accurate. A wrong date could send potential employers running in the other direction. It is unnecessary to include the day you started or the day you left.

Company Name

Include the full company name and abbreviation. Most companies are interested in hiring employees from their competitors and recruiters

If you are unsure of your dates of employment, call your former employer and request the information.

will conduct database searches using the name of the competitor as a search criterion. For example a recruiter from Toyota will conduct a search for employees who work for Honda.

If a previous employer has changed its name, include both names. For example: GUF, formerly Lansdowne Consultants Ltd.

Company Website

To make your resume more searchable and to provide a recruiter with more information about your previous employer, include the company web address.

Company Location

The company location should be listed on all resumes.

Title

As recruiters often conduct *job title* database searches, it is important to include both your full title and the abbreviation. As an example, Senior Vice President (SVP).

Functional Title

Unlike conventional resumes some Ugly Resumes include an additional line, the Functional Title. The purpose of the Functional Title is to increase both the number of *hits* and *ranking* a resume receives during a database search and to overcome hurtles candidates with unique, non-descriptive titles face.

As an example, Bob holds the unique non-descriptive title of North West Region Representative. This vague title sheds very little light on what he actually does. Is he a salesperson, part of the technical support staff or a manager? More importantly, it is very unlikely that a recruiter will conduct a search for "North West Region Representative" when he or she is trying to locate a sales person.

By adding the following Functional Title line,

Functional Title: Sales, Business Development, Account Manager, New Territory Development

Bob has not only clarified his job responsibilities but also increased the number of times his resume is viewed by recruiters.

The functional title line isn't necessary on all resumes. If you hold a commonly known, self-

Include all awards, achievements and accomplishments in your Job Responsibility section.

explanatory title such as: Teacher, CFO, Pediatric Nurse, etc then it is unnecessary to include this line.

Job Responsibilities

This is your opportunity to showcase your expertise! Don't simply list your responsibilities; rather paint a picture of your successes. Use plenty of action words (see Appendix C) and key words specific to your industry.

Reason for Leaving (Optional)

Companies do not like candidates who *job hop* (change jobs frequently). The appearance of job-hopping on a resume typically means immediately disqualification of the candidate. If you have held several jobs in a short amount of time and are the victim of downsizing, right-sizing, company closures, etc., then we strongly suggest you include the *reason for leaving* section under each job. As an example:

Reason for Leaving: Company went bankrupt, closed all North American facilities

Warning: This is not the place to try and defend a rightful termination. Potential employers do not want to hear you speak poorly of your previous employer. Some things are left best unsaid.

If you were terminated from a previous job because of a prohibited act, do not include this information on your resume. The interview is the appropriate time to discuss the situation.

viii] REFRENCES

This section requires the statement, *"Available upon Request"*.

Respect the privacy of your references and do not include their names and contact information on your resume. If a potential employer is interested in hiring you, he or she will request the names of your references at the appropriate time during the interview process and have you sign a release authorization.

ix] CITIZENSHIP

For various reasons, some companies will not sponsor work visas. If you are a foreign national who has obtained citizenship or the legal right to work in a country, it is important that you include this on your resume. If you do not include this information, your resume may be disqualified based on the wrongful assumption that you will require sponsorship for a work visa.

3. CREATE A BASIC INTRODUCTION EMAIL

It is important to write an effective introduction email that will accompany each resume submission. Like the profile, the introduction email is a mini commercial designed to entice the reader. Your introduction email should be customized for each job you apply to. It should not be too lengthy, but should be more than two sentences and contain the following:

i]   SALUTATION

Dear Mr. /Ms. Last Name (If you do not have a contact name, then address the reader as Dear Sir/Madam)

ii]   PURPOSE STATEMENT

This statement provides the employer with specific information about the position you are applying to. As employers typically have several advertised openings on different job boards, websites, print ads, etc, it is important to list the title of the job and where you found it. If you are submitting a general application, this statement is intended to provide information about where you would like to work in the company. If you

Don't use nicknames, if someone lists their contact name as Robert, then address them as "Robert", not "Bob" or "Rob".

Don't assume the person reading your resume is male, by addressing the reader as "Dear Sirs".

were referred to the recruiter by a mutual contact, then include that information in your purpose statement. As examples:

- *With reference to your advertised Human Resource Manager role on www.majorjobboard.com, I have attached my resume for your review.*

- *With reference, I have attached my resume for any job openings you may have in your customer service department in Vancouver.*

- *I was referred to you by Thomas Smith, Head of IT, at your Seattle location.*

iii]   BODY – PARAGRAPH 1

In the first paragraph summarize why you are a great fit for the position you are applying to. If you are submitting a general application, then summarize why you are a great candidate. Use the information found in your profile.

iv]   BODY – PARAGRAPH 2

In this paragraph, express your interest in the position and/or company and ask for a meeting with the hiring authority to further discuss your credentials and how they may benefit the hiring company.

Develop a system to manage your contacts and correspondence.

v] COMPLIMENTARY CLOSE

Like a formal letter, a complimentary close is required. This is a business correspondence not a letter to a friend, be selective on the close you choose. Examples of good closures include:

Regards | Kind Regards | Respectively | Sincerely

vi] SIGNATURE

Conclude your email with your first and last name and daytime telephone number.

As an example this is the introduction email, Jack Wiseman (see Case Study 1 – Appendix A) sent to Software Services International.

Dear Sir/ Madam,

With reference I have attached my resume for the Account Manager role advertised in The Local Trade Magazine.

Upon reviewing my resume, I am confident you will find that I am a great fit for the advertised position. For the past twelve years I have sold software and services to SMBs and Fortune 500 manufacturers. My hunter mentality has helped me find and close large multi-seat deals, exceeding annual quotas, winning business from competitors and developing

Most recruiters will instantly delete an email / cover letter addressed to someone else or a generic email blast to multiple recruiters. Take 30 seconds and customize each correspondence.

strong pipelines. My greatest career achievements included developing two extremely successful territories from scratch which exceeded the company's growth expectations. My proven track record and references support that I am an added value to any team.

I am very interested in pursuing an Account Manager role with Software Services International and would welcome an opportunity to speak with you further about how my credentials may be of benefit to your organization.

Regards,
Jack Wiseman
Home: 704-555-1111 Cell: 704-555-2222

TASKS:

Now that you have read Chapter Two, let's create your *Ugly Resume* and *introduction email*. If you already have a resume then reformat it as an *Ugly Resume*.

Remember, that your introduction email and profile on your Ugly Resume must be customized to meet the specific requirements of each job you apply to.

Using this chapter as a reference, create your Ugly Resume:

1. Open your word processing program - set your font style to *Arial*, font *size 11.* Leave all margins set to the manufacturer's standard settings.

2. Save the document as **Resume-Your Last Name, Your First Name**

3. Centered at the top of the page, enter your contact information:

FIRST NAME, LAST NAME
Home Address (*optional*)
Contact Telephone Number (s)
Email Address

For aesthetic reasons, some candidates prefer to increase the font size of their name.

4. *(If applicable)* Justified to the left, title (in capital letters) the next section **EDUCATION**. Enter your education history in the following format, starting with your most recent degree.

Year Graduated   **Name of School, Location**
                             Degree/Diploma, Area of Study

5. *(If applicable)* Justified to the left, title (in capital letters) the next section **LICENSES AND CERTIFICATIONS**. List your licenses and certifications in the following format:

License / Certification (Abbreviation)   **Year Completed**

6. Justified to the left, title (in capital letters) the next section **TECHNICAL SKILLS**. List your technical skills under the heading. For those of you who have multiple technical skills, we suggest creating two columns of skills.

7. *(If applicable)* Justified to the left, title (in capital letters) the next section **ADDITIONAL TRAINING**. List your training in the following format:

Year Completed   **Course Title**   **Name of Institution**

8. Justified to the left, title (in capital letters) the next section **EMPLOYMENT HISTORY**. Starting with your most recent employer, record your employment history as follows:

    MM/YY – Pres   **Name of Employer, City, Prov /State**
    www.webaddress.com
    Title:
    Functional Title: (*Optional*)

    Detail job responsibilities in point form. Use of plenty of descriptive words, see Appendix B for ideas

9. Justified to the left, title (in capital letters) the next section **REFERENCES**. Below the heading enter:

    Available upon Request

10. Justified to the left and inserted below your CONTACT INFORMATION and above EDUCATION, enter the heading **PROFILE** in capital letters. Highlight your career successes, pertinent experience, and education in dynamic statements using plenty of action words and industry key words.

As an example:

Certified PMP with more than four (4) years experience managing complex infrastructure projects

MBA who is well versed in Microsoft Unified Communications technologies

Successfully completed two multi-million projects on time and within budget

Recognized as leader with strong business acumen

11. Reread Chapter Two - Section 1 and 2 paying special attention to the Do's, Don'ts and Lessons.

12. Review your resume; can you improve on the content? If so, make the appropriate changes.

Save a second version of your resume as a .txt file. Be sure to open the .txt file and adjust your alignment.

Using Chapter Two – Section 3 as a reference, create your introduction email:

13. Open your word processing program - set your font style to *Arial,* font *size 11.* Leave all margins set to the manufacturer's standard settings.

14. Save the document as **Introduction Email**

15. Create your introduction email. Use your profile and our sample email as a reference.

16. Creating a well written resume and introduction email is hard work, you deserve some rest! Take an hour for yourself and do something you enjoy!

BUILD YOUR BRAND 50

DON'T FORGET YOUR FISHING POLE

CHAPTER 03

In today's sophisticated, technology driven, highly competitive employment market, a well crafted resume is not enough to land your next great job. You must stand out from the crowd by branding yourself as an exceptional, low risk, high yield employee that companies will line up to hire. In this chapter we will help you build your online and offline brand.

1. BUILD YOUR BRAND

Companies hire based on their business needs not the needs of candidates. Everyone's job - including your recruiters - is dispensable. In order to have your resume promoted and presented through the application process a candidate must fulfill an immediate business need and be considered a good investment.

Which candidates are considered good investments?

Candidates who have a proven track record of past successes and are predicted to produce high results are considered good investments. These candidates will consistently get interviews and land top jobs!

In order to secure your next great job, you must *brand* yourself as one of these candidates. Every resume, email, reference, conversation with recruiters and your online presence must support this image. Recruiters will not risk their professional reputations or jobs to promote mediocre candidates with questionable credentials to their superiors.

You must ensure that everything about you (*your brand*), says that you are an outstanding employee. In the previous chapter you created an Ugly Resume and introduction email which are an important part of your brand, but they are only part of the puzzle. In the following section we will help you complete your branding. You will:

i] BUILD YOUR ONLINE IMAGE

In today's technology driven recruiting world employers have more access to you both professionally and personally. To avoid costly hiring errors and waste valuable time on poor candidates, more and more recruiters use the Internet to research potential candidates prior to speaking to them. This means that with the help of the Internet, a recruiter may know:

> *What you look like*
> *Who your friends are*
> *Who your business associates are*
> *What your house looks like*
> *The names of your children*
> *The groups and organizations you belong to, etc*

It is extremely important to your brand - and successful job search - that you create a positive

EVERYTHING MATTERS!

The tiniest bit of online information may have recruiters running in the other direction. Be very selective about what you publish online.

online image. What does the Internet say about you? Ask yourself, is there something on your personal website or blog, Facebook, LinkedIN ™, Twitter or other social media sites and/or a dating site that may hinder your job search?

Does your online image depict a successful professional who will have a positive impact on a company or does it predict an upcoming guest appearance on a second-rate daytime talk show?

Clean up your online image. It is imperative that your online presence promotes your - *I am an outstanding employee* - claim! To avoid *guilt by association*, make all friend's lists and colleague lists private. Delete or make private personal photos.

Refrain from *negative online speak*, if you are unsatisfied with a former employer, a politician or a product you have recently purchased, don't broadcast your angst online. Potential employers will remember your *negative speaks* and not the skills and experience you can offer their organization.

Don't provide potential employers with a video resume. More and more job seekers are using *YouTube* or one of several video resume sites to create a self-promotion video. A video resume is

Create a profile on LinkedIN ™! Network profiles receive a fairly high page-rank in Google ™, this is a great way to influence what people learn about you.

a great marketing tool for job seekers who are applying to positions that will require them to be in front of the camera such as a performer, reporter or a public speaker.

For most candidates; however, we do not recommend a video resume for these reasons: 1) Video resumes allow companies to discriminate against you; 2) Your great credentials will be overshadowed by the clothes you wear, the sound of your voice, or even your hairstyle! 3) Professional video resume sites are often quite expensive; and 4) Many companies will not accept video resumes for fear of discrimination lawsuits.

As a final step to building your online brand, perform a simple Google ™, Yahoo ™ and bing™ search for *your first name, last name* - you may be surprised at what appears! Innocent information found online may prevent a recruiter from calling you.

ii]   RECORD AN APPROPRIATE PHONE MESSAGE

We recommend that you have a dedicated phone such as a cell phone, for your job search. Record a simple, professional voice message on all

If you can't speak freely or are in a noisy place, do not answer your phone - let your voicemail take the call. Accepting a call from a recruiter at your local noisy pub may send the wrong message!

phone lines you have provided potential employers with, for example:

"You have reached the voicemail of Brad Smith; I am unable to take your call. Please leave a message and I will call you back as soon as possible."

When recording your voice message speak clearly and use proper English. Do not play music or record spiritual versus; keep the message simple and professional.

iii] SELECT REFERENCES

Choose your references wisely. Most potential employers will request three professional references including at least one reference from a former manager. The more managers you have that support your - *I am an outstanding employee* - brand, the better it will be for your application.

Be sure to contact your potential references and ask permission to list their name as a reference. Don't assume that if someone agrees to be your reference that they are going to provide a glowing recommendation! Ask your references what they are going to say about you. If you are not satisfied with their answers, then it is time to list another reference.

Once you have chosen your references, confirm the spelling of their first and last name, current title, employer and contact number. Provide references only when asked by the potential hiring company and once you have signed a release authorization form.

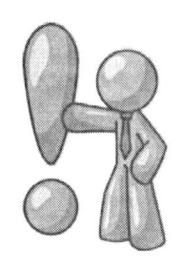

iv]   DRESS FOR SUCCESS

We cover this in greater detail in the interview section of the book; however, it is worth mentioning here too. During an interview, it is important that you dress for the job you want, not the job you have. It's easier to loosen a tie and take a jacket off than trying to produce one at the last minute. Regardless of how good you are or *"in Florida we don't wear ties"*, remember you are the one who needs the job. Short of wearing a tuxedo or a ball gown, you can never overdress for an interview.

See Chapter Six for more tips on dressing for success.

Due to litigation issues, many companies have strict policies which forbid managers from providing employee references. If your former employer happens to be one of these companies, ask your former manager if he/she will be comfortable providing "a personal reference" for you and then have the recruiter call him/her afterhours.

As a final note, positive branding is important because:

You can judge a book by its cover…
Prior to speaking to you, recruiters will form an opinion of you based on your resume, your email

address, where you attended school, companies you have worked for, titles you have held, your online image and your voicemail.

You can't win a race if you're not in it...

Good recruiters are trained to go for the "no" early in the interview process so valuable time and resources aren't wasted on unqualified candidates. This means that recruiters will be looking for reasons to disqualify your application early in the candidate selection process. Don't disqualify yourself before you have had a chance to speak with the company.

It's easier to run downhill than climb up...

During an interview, a recruiter will view you through tainted glasses. As mentioned above, an opinion of you was formed long before your first conversation. This opinion (good or bad) taints each interaction with the recruiter. Everything you say during the interview process will further substantiate the recruiter's opinion.

Six degrees of separation can either hurt you or help you...

We are all connected by six degrees of separation. Meaning, there is currently someone within your reach that can help you land your next great job. The problem is most people in your personal and professional network will not risk their good reputations recommending a wayward individual. To maximize your current network, you must brand yourself as an all-star that your friends, family and business colleagues will proudly recommend.

TASKS:

Now that you have read Chapter Three, let's create your brand.

1. Conduct a personal online audit of all your current professional and social networking site accounts. (*Refer to Step One Build Your Online Image*)

2. Conduct a Google ™, Yahoo ™ and bing™ search on your name. If you discover unflattering information, then contact the source and ask to have the information removed.

3. If you do not belong to a social networking site, we recommend you join two today. LinkedIN ™ (www.LinkedIN .com) and Facebook (www.facebook.com) are popular choices. If you are concerned about your online identity, then list your name as *confidential*. Be sure to include your current job title or occupation, and previous employer's names as many recruiters will use these key words when conducting searches for candidates.

4. If the networking site allows, join groups that are related to your industry. This will give

you access to hiring managers and recruiters who also belong to these groups.

5. Record your voice message (*Refer to Step Two – Record an Appropriate Voice Message*).

6. Enter the names of your references.

    a)

    b)

    c)

7. Contact each of these people, ask permission to use them as a reference, confirm that they will give you a positive recommendation and confirm their current title and contact information.

8. Ensure that your interview clothes are ready.

9. Reduce your stress and spend half of the day doing something physical and preferably outside.

JOB SEARCH ETIQUETTE	62
WHERE RECRUITERS ADVERTISE JOBS	63
HOW ONLINE JOB BOARDS WORK	71
DISPELLING THE MYTHS ABOUT HOW COMPANIES RECRUIT & HOW TO OVERCOME THEM	76

LET'S GO FISHING

CHAPTER 04

Now that you are armed with an exceptional resume, an outstanding introductory email and a brand that will have employers lining up to hire you, it is time to find a job! In this chapter, we will take you behind the recruiter's desk to show you where top companies advertise and how recruiters look for candidates on job boards. We will also show you how to find the major or niche job boards and dispel some common myths about recruiting.

1. JOB SEARCH ETIQUETTE

Before we begin discussing where recruiters advertise jobs, it is important review job search etiquette. A certain amount of etiquette is paramount to any successful job search. Here are some basic rules of the game.

- Be polite and professional at all times. Even if the recruiter uses inappropriate language or slang during your conversation, always remain professional.

- Do not refer to a recruiter by a nickname unless the recruiter has given you permission to do so.

- Do not provide too much personal information, such as *"I am recently divorced, the bank has taken my home and my kids hate me"*. Recruiters do not want to hear this information. Giving too much personal information may prevent your application from moving forward.

- Do not over-embellish your skills, at some point you will be required to use them.

- Always send follow up thank you emails.

Etiquette is very important. When it comes down to a company deciding between two equally skilled applicants, the company will always choose the person who left a positive impression on them.

- Don't *over-contact* a recruiter. Refer to the Follow-Up Rules detailed in Chapter Seven.

- If you discover the name of a recruiter on a personal networking site, do not contact them on their personal email. Call or email them at work only.

2. WHERE RECRUITERS ADVERTISE JOBS

Diminishing recruiting budgets and limited internal resources have led companies to become more selective as to where they advertise their available job openings. It is estimated that only 20% of the nation's available jobs are actually advertised! In the next chapter, we will share the secrets of tapping into the other 80% of available jobs. For now, let's focus on the advertised openings. Often companies use the following places to advertise:

i] MAJOR JOB BOARDS

These websites serve as a general purpose job board, advertising all sorts of positions from janitors to CEOs. Employers pay a fee to access candidate resumes and post available positions online. The sites are free for candidates to use.

At the time this book was written, there were three major job boards used by employers: *www.monster.com* | *www.careerbuilder.com* | *www.yahoohotjobs.com*

As the Internet and today's business climate is ever-changing, these job boards may be superseded by the next great thing by the time this book is printed. To find the largest job boards, we suggest conducting Google™, bing™ and Yahoo™ searches using the following key words:

- "major" and "job" and "board"
- "largest" and "job" and "board"
- "popular" and "job" and "board"
- "top" and "job" and "boards"
- "biggest" and "job" and "boards"

See Appendix D for a list of current job boards.

Hint: Most major job boards allow candidates to conceal their identity. If you choose to make your profile confidential, ensure that you also delete your name from the resume you download.

RE: Confidential Profiles and job boards.

If you choose to make your profile confidential, then do not include an email address that reveals your identity such as: Firstname.lastname@currentemployer.com. Instead choose an obscure email address such as: 123ab@freemail.com

Hint: *Be forewarned that some companies do not have an official system for handling confidential resumes. Often these resumes are set aside and not entered into the normal recruiting system where job seekers are tracked by their first and last name. If you make your resume confidential you take a chance that your resume may get lost.*

ii] NATIONAL, LOCAL AND EMPLOYMENT NEWSPAPERS

Although advertising in newspapers has quickly become a thing of the past, some companies still use this method to attract candidates. Don't dismiss the classifieds!

iii] CORPORATE WEBSITE

Many companies have a career section on their corporate website where internal positions are posted. This page may also contain information about the company's application process and the benefits of working for the employer.

iv] NICHE JOB BOARDS

These are specialized job boards. Both employers who post jobs on these sites and candidates who post their resumes to these sites share a common interest.

Your local library is a great place to find national, local and employment newspapers.

Here are some examples of niche job boards:

- *www.dice.com (specializes in the technology industry)*
- *www.net-temps (specializes in temporary employment postings)*
- *www.medhunters.com (specializes in the medical industry)*

To find niche job boards for your industry, conduct the following Google ™, bing™ and Yahoo ™ searches

- *"job" and "your industry"*
- *"job" and "functional title"*
- *"job board" and "your industry"*

These searches will produce a list of job openings and where they are found, including niche sites.

See Appendix D for a more detailed list of Niche job boards.

v] STATE/FEDERAL EMPLOYMENT SITES

Most government employment agencies have websites where candidates can download their resumes for free and search available job openings.

Sometimes it's easier to use Meta/Mega web sites that instantaneously search all job boards. To find them do a Google ™ search using the key words; "mega meta job boards", "top 100 job board", "ultimate job search boards", "top job search engines" or try the following sites: Indeed™, Simplyhired™, Careerjet, JobSniper.

vi] EXECUTIVE JOB BOARDS

These job boards are geared toward professionals who earn more than $100K per annum. Job seekers are typically charged a fee to use the job board and have access to six figure positions that are usually not posted on other sites. Here are some examples of executive job boards:

- *www.theladders.com*
- *www.6figurejobs.com*
- *www.higherbracket.ca*

If you can, contact a recruiter from your former employer and ask her where she posts jobs; chances are similar companies (who would be interested in your skills) are using the same job boards.

vii] SPECIALTY MAGAZINES/INDUSTRY NEWSLETTERS

When seeking a specialized employee, recruiters will often advertise in industry specific magazines and newsletters. These positions may not be advertised on major job boards.

viii] PROFESSIONAL ASSOCIATIONS

Some associations have a career section on their website, while smaller organizations may have a local bulletin board in their office. Regardless, if you belong to a professional association, it would behoove you to contact them regarding available job opportunities.

ix]   ALUMNI

Well organized alumni groups have career sites where alumni and employers can connect. Often employers have a preference for graduates from a certain school and/or program and will give these job seekers preferential ranking over other applicants. These employers will often advertise on the alumni sites.

x]   PROFESSIONAL NETWORKING SITES

These social media sites are designed for business networking. Professionals network with one another to sell products or services, stay in touch with colleagues, and recruiters actively use these sites to attract candidates and advertise current openings. One of the more popular professional networking sites is *www.LinkedIN™.com*; however, there are other professional sites used by recruiters. To discover these sites conduct the following Google ™, bing™ and Yahoo ™ key word searches:

- "business" and "networking sites"
- "professional" and "networking sites"
- "professional" and "social networks"

When speaking to the Association or Alumni Office, ask the representative if he or she knows of a good recruiter or hiring manager in your field.

Many networking sites allow you to add a brief caption describing what you are doing; this is a great place to advertise that you are seeking employment.

Here is a partial list of the more popular networking sites:

www.spoke.com | www.LinkedIN ™.com | www.plaxo.com | www.talkbiznow.com | www.xing.com | www.naymz.com

When you create your profile on any networking site, ensure that you properly brand yourself as an outstanding employee.

xi] SOCIAL NETWORKING SITES

These social media sites are places where friends come together. Typically less formal than professional networking sites, these sites are often used by recruiters to find suitable candidates. Popular social networking sites are Facebook, Twitter and Myspace. As previously mentioned - consistent messaging.

To gain access to hiring managers and recruiters, join as many industry specific groups as you can. If the site has discussion groups, read all discussion feeds, often recruiters will post jobs there.

xii] OUTSOURCING COMPANIES

When some corporations downsize, they hire outsourcing companies to help their displaced workforce secure employment. If you are fortunate enough to have this resource, then utilize it! Often these companies will have job boards available to third party recruiters and corporate recruiters where they can post jobs and search the candidate database. It is in the best interest of the outsourcing company to get you hired - utilize their resources.

xiii] TRAINING / CERTIFICATION / LICENSING CENTERS

Often recruiters will contact training, certification and licensing centers with job openings. Some of these centers have online job boards for their graduates, while others have a more informal system for posting jobs such as a bulletin board.

xiv] ONLINE CLASSIFIEDS

There are several online classified sites where consumers buy and sell merchandise, businesses advertise services, recruiters post job openings, and candidates post resumes. Some of the more popular online classified sites are:

www.craigslist.org | www.kijiji.com | www.webcrawler.com www.Google ™.com/base (currently still beta but may become the largest classified site)

Due to security issues, we recommend that you do not post your resume on an online classified site.

To find additional online classifieds, try the following key word searches on Google ™, bing™ and Yahoo ™:

- "classifieds for job" or "(city) classifieds for jobs"

xv] BILLBOARDS, PARK BENCHES, OUTSIDE SIGNS, BUSES, ETC

Some companies turn to more public forms of advertisement such as busses or billboards. Always keep your eyes open as you don't know where your next great job might be advertised.

3. A CLOSER LOOK AT HOW ONLINE JOB BOARDS WORK

Now that we have reviewed all the different places employers advertise jobs, let's take a closer look at the popular online job boards. An online job board is a database of job openings and candidate resumes. By entering certain search criteria, employers are able to find suitable candidates and candidates are able to locate suitable job openings.

i] GET NOTICED

To be found by a recruiter on a job board, you must understand *how* a recruiter will look for you. On most job boards, the recruiter is able to search on a string of keywords to locate a candidate. These keywords are often related to a candidate's:

- *Education (degree achieved and/ or school attended)*
- *Training/certification/licenses/specific designations*
- *Specific technical skills*
- *Job title*
- *Current/ previous employer*
- *Job responsibilities*
- *Intangible skills*

Recruiters are also able to add such search criteria as:

- *Location*
- *Industry*
- *Part-time/full-time employment*

- *Legal eligibility to work without visa sponsorship*

- *Compensation level*

- *The age of the resume (How long ago was the resume entered into the system?)*

The more closely your resume and profile match the recruiter's search criteria, the higher your candidate file will rank on the search. Ideally, you want your resume to be one of the first ten resumes found. But how do you achieve this? Although nothing can guarantee your ranking, you can take certain steps to better your odds, such as:

- Ensure that your account profile contains as much information as possible. Do not leave any section blank.

- Ensure that your resume contains plenty of key words related to your industry. Be sure to include both the full name and abbreviation of technical skills, certifications, degrees and employer (if applicable), etc.

- Ensure that your resume contains the *Functional Title* line.

ii] FIND A JOB

Job boards allow job seekers to enter search criteria (key words) to locate suitable job openings and offer the ability to apply online. Many job boards also list the most recent job openings on their homepage and will email job seekers new jobs as they are posted by employers.

iii] HOW TO APPLY FOR A JOB ONLINE

The process for applying to a job online differs from job board to job board; however, most have an *"apply"* button on the job opening that will walk you through the process of applying online. Remember:

Customize!

Customize the profile on your Ugly Resume to meet the requirements of the job. Clearly explain to the recruiter why you are the best person for the job. See Appendix B to see how to customize your profile.

Customize!

If the job board allows a message to be written to the recruiter, cut and paste your introduction email here.

Be sure to customize the introduction email to match the job being applied to.

Follow Up!

The most effective way to ensure a recruiter reviews your application is to follow up. When you contact the hiring authority simply state that you are following up on the status of your application for (provide details about the job) and express your interest in the position and the company.

If you do not have a contact name for the position, refer to the upcoming chapter "Finding Secret Fishing Holes" – How to Connect with Key Decision Makers.

When applying online many corporate websites will provide you with an automated response that your resume has been received. This does mean that anyone has reviewed it, rather it is a confirmation that your resume is in the big black hole! Unless you speak with someone at the company about the specific job, assume that your resume has not been reviewed by a recruiter or hiring manager.

Following up with hiring authorities may be a daunting task, but well worth it. We have worked with large companies whose recruiting systems are so disorganized that often managers don't even get to see all the qualified candidates who apply.

4. DISPELLING THE MYTHS ABOUT HOW COMPANIES RECRUIT & HOW TO OVERCOME THEM

Knowing where companies advertise jobs is only part of the battle; you must also understand how companies recruit top candidates. Don't assume you know. Wrongful assumptions could stall your application forever! Here are some common myths about how companies recruit and ways to overcome them.

i] MYTH

A company's website is an accurate depiction of their current openings.

REALITY: In an ideal world this would be true; however, often overworked recruiters or hiring managers do not have the time to enter the new jobs online or delete the old ones. Most companies have *unofficial* or *unadvertised* job openings. If the right candidate applied, the recruiter would pursue his or her resume.

ACTION: Submit a general application to the company. Find the head of recruiting or hiring manager and pick up the phone and call them to follow up on your application.

ii]   MYTH

All companies use the major job boards to search for candidates and post job openings.

REALITY: Most companies operate on a limited recruiting budget. Advertising job openings and searching the candidate databases of the major job boards can become quite expensive. To offset recruiting costs many companies choose to post openings on their company website or on niche job boards.

ACTION: Be creative in your job search. Think *"where would a recruiter look for someone like me"* and make sure you are there!

iii]   MYTH

My resume was properly downloaded to the job board or the hiring company's website.

REALITY: Depending on the technology used by the job board or website, such things as complicated fonts, text boxes, graphics, etc, may actually prevent your resume from being downloaded or may only partially download it.

ACTION: Use the Ugly Resume format found in this book for all online applications.

iv] MYTH

Someone will actually look at my resume.

REALITY: Unless your resume contains certain key words, it is unlikely that it will ever by viewed by a person.

ACTION: Ensure that your resume contains many key words, acronyms and phrases. Also include a function title.

v] MYTH

The Company will see that I am a perfect fit for the position.

REALITY: Don't assume that the person reading your resume understands what you do and shares your vision match. You must clearly articulate why you are a fit for the position.

ACTION: Include a profile at the beginning of your resume which clearly defines why you are a perfect person for the position.

vi] MYTH

Placing my resume on all the major job boards will guarantee more interviews.

REALITY: Not all companies use the major boards.

ACTION: The best way to guarantee more interviews is to apply directly to companies that are in your industry and actively market yourself to hiring managers at these companies.

vii] MYTH

I will be hired based on my education and past work history.

REALITY: Although, these two things will likely get you an interview, but if you can't sell yourself to the company and explain how you are going to improve their business, then you won't get hired.

ACTION: When creating the profile on your resume and during an interview always ask the question "what is the benefit to the hiring company?" Their decision to hire you is not about you and your needs; it is about them and their needs.

viii] MYTH

If I send my resume to a company several times it will get noticed and they will see how interested I am in their company.

REALITY: Although the company may notice your resume, it will not be for a good reason.

ACTION: Send your resume once, and use our follow up strategy outlined in Chapter Seven.

ix] MYTH

Most companies do not check references or verify education.

REALITY: Recruiters are judged on the quality, caliber and work ethic of the candidates they hire. Be assured they will do all their homework before presenting a candidate to upper management.

ACTION: Ensure that all educational credentials are accurate on your resume. Ensure that your references know that they are your references and will say positive things about you.

x] MYTH

If a company likes my resume, they will call me to schedule an interview.

REALITY: In today's technology driven employment market, recruiters are bombarded with resumes. Although a recruiter may notice your resume and have the best intentions to call you – your application may get lost in the paperwork (or email work).

ACTION: Use our follow up strategy outlined in Chapter Seven to properly follow up on the resume submission.

xi] MYTH

Companies won't remember me applying for previous jobs or interviewing with a different hiring manager.

REALITY: Inexpensive storage solutions, advanced software programs and discrimination law suits ensure that most if not all correspondence and interviewing notes are recorded and easily accessible.

ACTION: If you have a bad track record or experience with a company, don't waste your time applying again. Chances are you are not going to get hired.

xii] MYTH

I interviewed with a company several months ago, it went very well and the manager wanted to offer me a job, but a hiring freeze was enacted. The hiring manager will call me with the hiring freeze is lifted.

REALITY: If you don't follow up with the manager she may assume you have found other work, or may have forgotten about you, lost your number, etc - it is worth a follow up call.

ACTION: Follow up with the manager until you get a definitive "no".

xiii] MYTH

It is illegal for a hiring company to use social networking sites to find out information about candidates.

REALITY: Not true. Savvy recruiters will often conduct Google ™ searches or search social media sites to find out information about candidates before they call them. Information found on these sites could be very detrimental to your job search.

ACTION: Ensure that you have properly branded yourself as a great candidate.

xiv] MYTH

Hiring authorities don't accept phone calls from candidates.

REALITY: A hiring manager may be too busy to take your call, but a well composed voice message about your interest in a position will certainly raise your application above other candidates.

ACTION: Call the hiring manager and express your interest in the position either personally or via a voice message.

TASKS:

1. List 10 job boards you plan to use during your job search.

2. If applicable, contact your Alumni Office and see if they have a job board available for their Alumni.

3. If applicable, contact all associations you belong to and inquire about the availability of a job board for members.

4. If applicable, contact all training centers you have attended and inquire about the availability of a job board for graduates.

PROACTIVE JOB SEARCH STRATEGIES	88
PASSIVE JOB SEARCH STRATEGIES	94
CONNECT WITH KEY DECISION MAKERS	97

FINDING SECRET FISHING HOLES

CHAPTER 05

You won't find a sign in the middle of the river that says "Secret Fishing Spot – Thousands of Fish Live Here". But the fish are there. It is estimated that about 80% of job openings are never advertised. This means that 100% of applicants are applying to only 20% of the available jobs! In this chapter we will teach you how to use both proactive and passive job search strategies to uncover the hidden job market.

1. PROACTIVE JOB SEARCH STRATEGIES

Proactive job search strategies will require many of you to step outside of your comfort zone, by either picking up the phone or sending an email to an absolute stranger and requesting help. It is important to your successful job search that you set aside your pride, fear of rejection and follow these strategies. The reality of your job search is, you will receive more *no's* than *yes'*. But you only require one *yes* to change your situation.

Before we begin exploring the hidden job market using proactive job search strategies, there are key points we want you to remember.

Companies make decisions to hire people based on business needs, not personal needs. If a recruiter fails to respond to your email or does not return your phone call, don't take it personally! Pick up the phone and call them again, they may not have received your message or may have been too busy to call or email you back. If they fail to respond again, it means that they do not have a business need for your credentials.

Companies have policies. If a receptionist refuses to provide you with a contact name or connect you

It isn't always the most qualified candidate who gets the job; rather, it is the candidate who connects with the right person at the right time.

directly to a recruiter, he is following company policy and is doing his job. Don't wallow in rejection, move on and contact someone else or try a different approach!

Even when you feel that you have exhausted all possible leads, take a breath and keep going. You haven't exhausted all leads until you have found your next great job. Ask yourself what's scarier, asking for a name or not being able to cover the mortgage?

In the following pages, we have detailed the proactive job search strategies that will help you uncover the hidden job market.

i] NETWORKING

Job search experts agree that networking is the most effective way to find a job. This process involves developing and maintaining connections with people who may be able to help in your search for new employment. For the best results, you need to fully utilize both your personal and professional networks.

Tap into your personal network

Your personal network consists of friends, family, members of your church, your child's soccer coach, your yoga instructor, neighbors, etc.

Tap into your professional network

Your professional network consists of both former and current: coworkers, customers, vendors, instructors, trainers, etc.

ii]   JOB / CAREER FAIRS

The second proactive job search strategy requires you to attend job fairs. A job fair is an opportunity for job seekers to meet directly with employers. Typically employers will accept resumes, hand-out business cards, provide a list of available openings and conduct brief interviews of top candidates. Job fairs are usually advertised in local newspapers, radio stations and newscasts.

iii]   ACTIVELY MARKET YOURSELF

The third proactive job search strategy requires you to actively market yourself to third party recruiters who specialize in your industry and hiring authorities at companies where you would like to work. Before you begin marketing yourself to these professionals, you must have a clear understanding of *why* you are a great

Regardless of how insignificant or weak you believe a lead to be, FOLLOW UP on it! Don't forget to thank your contacts for their assistance both verbally and in an email.

employee and *how* you can benefit a company. Not unlike a large corporation who sells the features and benefits of a product to consumers, you must be willing to sell the features and benefits of *yourself* to a potential employer. This process involves directly calling hiring authorities and *pitching yourself* to them. To be successful, you must create an effective voice message and opening line for when the hiring authority answers the phone.

This is not a script, you need to find your own voice and create your own message. The key to success is constantly tweaking your message until you find what works for you.

As an example, review the following phone message to Jim James the Director of Sales at INITECH:

Jim,

I know this is an unorthodox way of contacting you - however, being in a sales role for the past 5 years I have continuously exceeded my sales quota and would be very interested in talking to you about your current hiring needs. Do you have some availability later on this week to meet?

My name is Steve Rawlins and you can reach me at 519.555.1234. I will also follow up with an email containing my contact information.

Let's deconstruct the voice mail:

Jim,

I know this is an unorthodox way of contacting you

Humility works better than overconfidence, even for a sales role

...being in a sales role for the past 5 years

Generalize your experience, peak his interest

...I have continuously exceeded my sales quota

Always *emphasize the benefit to them* remember the acronym WIIFT (What's In It For Them)

...and would be interested in talking to you about your current hiring needs. Do you have some availability later on this week to meet?

The best way to positively influence your application is to get a meeting with the decision maker. You need to ask for the meeting! Busy managers will not volunteer their time.

My name is Steve Rawlins and you can reach me at 519.555.1234

Never start with your name and contact information. Unless you are Matt Lauer, your name alone will not entice the manager to

Always have your commercial message in front of you. You will be extremely nervous and if you try to "wing it" you may come across sounding awkward or incompetent.

continue to listen to your message. Managers are typically bombarded with calls from sales people and are programmed to delete messages instantly and cut phone calls short with these people; you don't want to be mistaken for a salesperson.

I will also follow up with an email containing my contact info.

If you don't hear from them within the hour, follow up with an email summarizing your voice mail. If you don't hear from him within three days, call again.

I look forward to your call. .

Use the power of suggestion.

If the key decision maker answers the phone, Steve could use a version of his voice message as an opening line -

I know this is an unorthodox way of contacting you - however, being in a sales role for the past 5 years I have continuously exceeded my sales quota and would be very interested in talking to you about your current hiring needs? Do you have a few minutes to talk right now or can we schedule a time to meet this week?

When speaking directly to a key decision maker, ensure that you always pass along your contact information. Make it easy for them to remember and contact you.

2. PASSIVE JOB SEARCH STRATEGIES

As detailed in the previous pages, proactive job search strategies require continuous action on your part to locate a job. Passive job search strategies involve initial action at the beginning and the job eventually finding you!

i] ONLINE JOB BOARDS

There are hundreds of online boards available to job seekers. Despite the claims by some of these sites, it is impossible to predict which one will generate a response from a recruiter. We suggest that you create a profile and download your resume to all the major job boards (Monster® Careerbuilder™, Hotjobs™), then move to niche (geographic and/or industry specific) job boards. *(See Appendix D)*

Hint: When choosing a job board, look at the available positions first before you create a profile and download your resume. You want to post your resume on a job board that already has several advertised positions in your field.

Hint: To locate industry and geographical specific job boards, try the following Google ™, bing™ and

Yahoo ™ key word searches: "jobs" and "your area of expertise" or" area of expertise" and "city or state you are interested in".

Hint: Listen to your instincts. If you have a bad feeling about posting your private information on a certain job board, then don't do it! Although most job boards are legitimate and respect the privacy of their clientele, other sites have been known to sell job seeker's personal information to third parties.

ii] NETWORKING SITES

These social media sites are a popular way for companies to connect with potential customers and to actively recruit new employees for minimal or no cost. As mentioned earlier, individuals use these sites to: connect with business associates, fellow alumni and friends, share information and engage in discussions with like-minded individuals, network with recruiters and hiring managers, apply to advertised job openings and try to create potential business opportunities.

As a job seeker you can also leverage these sites to:

- *Find the name of the hiring manager or decision maker at a specific company and network with them in a more relaxed setting.*

- *Increase your web visibility. Most of these sites allow search engines to make your profile information available for search engines to index.*

- *Learn more about the individual interviewing you. You may have likeminded interests which may help ease an interview.*

iii] RESUME DISTRIBUTION SERVICES

Resume distribution services blast resumes to recruiters on a daily or weekly basis. This service is free for recruiters but candidates pay a nominal fee. Like any other industry, there are good and bad resume distributions services. We recommend you get a referral from a family member, friend or coworker who has used a resume distribution service.

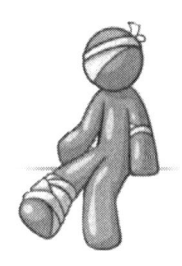

Regarding resume distribution services; don't just pay the asking fee and download your Ugly Resume without having done extensive homework on their services and references!

3. CONNECT WITH KEY DECISION MAKERS

The best way to uncover the hidden job market is to speak to the key decision makers *(people who have the authority to hire)* in an organization. Connecting with these people may be easier than you ever thought possible. It is as straightforward as finding out the name of the person and his or her contact information and then making a phone call or connecting online.

i] WHO IS THE KEY DECISION MAKER?

You will want the name of a recruiter within the organization or the name of the manager who heads up the department you are interested in working for. Think about your current or previous employer, what was your manager's title? What are alternative titles he or she may hold? The following sources will help you uncover the names of the key decision makers.

Believe it or not, often it is easier to get information (a name) from people at the top of the organization rather than at the bottom.

- **Telephone:** The easiest way to find out the information you require is to pick up the phone, call the company that you are interested in working for and ask to speak to the person who is in charge of *your area of expertise.*

- **Networking:** Contact people within your professional and personal networks and ask them if they know of anyone who works at *the company you are interested in.*

- **Online Searches**: The Internet is a great source for company information. Try the following Google ™, Yahoo ™ and bing™ key word searches :

  "manager" , *"company you are interested in"*

  "vice president", *"company you are interested in"*

  "recruiter" , *"company you are interested in"*

  Record the names of all the people you find who work for the company.

- **Networking Sites:** These sites will prove to be a valuable source of information. Use several networking sites to carry out your research. Conduct searches for the name of the company you are interest in working for. From the results, record the names and contact information of the managers. If appropriate, you may

When asked by the gatekeeper about the nature of your call, be honest and explain that it is regarding a personal business matter.

connect with them online through the networking site. If you are unable to locate a manager, then copy down the names of several employees.

- **Company Website**: Often companies will include press releases or corporate articles on their website. Search these documents, you may find the name of the person you are looking for. Record the names of all the people you find who work for the company.

- **Professional Associations**: If you are a member of a professional association, then you likely have access to their membership list. Search this list for anyone who works for the company you are interested in. Be sure to record the names of all the people you find who work for the company.

- **Chamber of Commerce:** Depending on the size of the organization, your local Chamber of Commerce may be a great resource for contact details. Record the names of all the people you find who work for the company.

When targeting specific companies ask current employees for the name of the hiring manager; most people will be happy to help you out.

- **Employee Referral Programs:** Most companies pay existing employees a lump sum of money for referring a job seeker who gets hired. Previously, we asked you to record the names of all employees you found at a given company. Now we want you to contact them and ask for the name of the hiring manager. Believe it or not, most people will gladly provide the information. The employee will also benefit because you become a referral, making them eligible for an employee referral bonus!

ii] WHAT IS THE KEY DECISION MAKER'S CONTACT INFORMATION?

Let's assume from the previous exercise, you were only able to uncover a name of the key decision maker, but no contact information. Use the following methods to find his or her contact information:

Call: Again, the easiest way to get information is to call the company and ask. If you are unable to retrieve the information from the receptionist, call after hours. Most companies have an automated attendant phone system that will allow you to connect to the key decision maker's extension and reveal the person's extension number.

Search: If the phone method is unsuccessful, then use the Internet. To begin, simply conduct a Google ™, Yahoo ™ and bing™ search for *"the person's full name and company name"*. If your search results fail to produce a contact telephone number or email address, then it is time to use a little bit of logic and luck!

Most companies have an email protocol, meaning that all of their emails follow a certain format i.e. – *firstname.lastname@company.com*. For example, let's assume you are seeking Liz Pappa's email address at The Big Company. Conduct a Google ™, Yahoo ™ and bing™ search for "@thebigcompany.com". The search results will produce email addresses of individuals who work at The Big Company. In our example, the results produced:

bbrown@thebigcompany.com
hhanson@thebigcompany.com
tthomas@thebigcompany.com

Based on the results, it is reasonable to conclude that Liz Pappa's email address is lpappa@thebigcompany.com. This strategy

Don't stalk key decision makers! If you try to connect with an individual on one networking site don't go to another networking site, their blog or worse, their personal site and attempt to connect with them again!

doesn't always work, but more often than not job seekers have great success with this method.

iii] CONTACT

Once you have the manager's or recruiter's contact information, call them or send them an email expressing your interest in working for their employer. Also confirm that you are speaking with the correct person, if you are not, ask for a referral.

TASKS:

1. In the space provided, create a voice message and the opening line you will use when networking with hiring authorities. Refer to the profile on your Ugly Resume where you have highlighted your key accomplishments for inspiration. Remember, both the message and opening line should highlight your skills, focus on the employer's needs (*not yours*), and entice the employer to speak to you.

What recruiters look for	106
Ace the interview – do's and don'ts	107
Follow up	113
How much are you worth?	115
Offer negotiations	116
How to accept/decline offers	118

LAND YOUR TROPHY FISH

CHAPTER 06

Congratulations! Your hard work and determination have paid off and you have an interview! Whether you will be speaking to a recruiter on the phone, via video-conferencing or in person, this is your opportunity to showcase your expertise and land your next great job. In this chapter, we help you identify what recruiters look for, avoid common interviewing pitfalls and negotiate what you're worth.

1. WHAT RECRUITERS LOOK FOR

The approach the interviewer takes to interviewing will be as varied as the number of companies and recruiters you meet with. Some interviewers are very structured and will read verbatim pre-determined questions to you, while others will follow a more relaxed conversational approach. Despite the approach taken by an interviewer, all are screening for the following:

MQ – Do you have the minimum qualifications (education, years experience, technical skills, etc) to do the job?

Personality Fit – Will you fit into the corporate culture? Do you possess the proper attitude, character and values?

Ability to Deliver – Can you deliver results that will make you a success story? Do you have a track record of success?

Risk Factor – Have you proven yourself as a low risk employee? Has your career followed a logical progression, can you rationalize your gaps in employment? How confident were your answers?

Make no mistake - an interview is a sales call. You have been given half an hour to sell yourself to the recruiter. By bringing every answer back to WIIFT (What's In It For Them), you will win the recruiter over.

2. ACE THE INTERVIEW – DO'S AND DON'TS

First impressions are lasting impressions! For both telephone interviews and in person interviews, follow these guidelines:

Do:

- Dress for the job you want, not the job you have
- Dress conservative. If you have tattoos or body piercings, cover them up. Don't wear revealing clothing
- Solid color clothing is best, dark colors preferred
- Limit jewelry
- Wear polished shoes
- Have clean, manicured nails
- Conservative hair styles are preferred
- Chew breath mints or use mouth spray prior to the meeting, no gum chewing! A cow chewing its cud, doesn't leave a positive impression on a hiring authority

During the interview, "be in the now!" Too often candidates are focused on rehearsing potential answers in their mind then focusing on what's currently being asked.

- If offered a coffee, accept it. Coffee will often mask any bad breath your body produces as part of a *fight or flight* parasympathetic response

- Listen carefully to the interviewers questions and provide precise answers referencing your resume

- Stay calm and don't rush to answer a question. Think about your answer before blurting out something.

- Don't assume you understand the question. If you are not 100% certain of what's being asked, ask for the question to be elaborated on

- Practice interviewing, rehearse your story

- Have a general understanding of the job description and requirements of the position prior to the interview

- Put together a list of your strengths and weaknesses. You will likely be asked to list one or two weakness', ensure your weakness' become strength, as an example, "I over obsess about the details, on a positive notes it helps in my role as an auditor."

- Speak clearly in proper English, do not use slang or profanity

- Have your resume in front of you, memorize it and ensure you can talk to every point listed on it

- Tell the truth, if you don't know the answer to a question, admit that you don't know

- Research the company and know the basic facts about their business and the industry they are in including: type of business the company conducts, size of company, locations and other facts relevant to the position

- Always have a list of questions to ask the interviewer. Recruiters love to talk and it will change the dynamic of interview if you can get them to talk about themselves. The easiest way to do that is to ask questions like, "What has your experience been like working for …?"

- Ask about next steps in the interview process, timeframe, etc

An interview is your opportunity to evaluate the company. At the end of the interview, ask yourself "do I want to work here"?

Some hiring authorities may experience anxiety during the interview as well.

- Confirm your interest in the position and the value you will bring to the company

- Smile (even during a phone interview, smiling will change the tone of your voice and project a positive image to the interviewer)

- Be available or arrive 15 minutes early for the interview

- Only answer what is asked, do not reveal a lot of personal information. Even if you think you made a connection with the interviewer, you didn't. Their job is to be nice and hire the best candidate, not the one who needed a new friend

- Thank the interviewer

Do Not:

- Wear cologne or perfume to the interview

- Accept calls from a cell phone or answer call waiting during a telephone interview

- Speak ill or derogatory of former employers

- Divulge confidential information about your current/former employer or offer up trade secrets and client lists

- Smoke in the car before an interview. Most non smokers hate the smell or have sensitivities to smoke

- Interrupt the interviewer when he or she is speaking

- Make sexual advances or flirt with your interviewer

This is NOT the time to start experimenting! Vanilla is the flavor of choice. Unless you walk on water, you can't wear Birkenstocks to an interview.

To help prepare for an interview, conduct a Google ™, Yahoo ™ and bing™ search using the following key words:

"*interview*" and the "*name of the company you are interviewing with*". There are several sites where applicants share interviewing experiences about companies. These sites may provide valuable insight for your upcoming interview including specific questions you may be asked.

If you are fortunate enough to be working with a good third party recruiter, he/she should be able to provide valuable interviewing advice regarding the types of questions that will be asked, details about the interviewer and the company.

Regardless of the recruiter's interviewing style, you will likely be asked a version of the following questions:

- Why did you leave/or want to leave your last job?

- Why would you be a good fit for this role?

- What are some of your strengths and weakness'?

- How much money do you want? (*We address this further on in the chapter*)

- What do you know about our company? (not only product portfolio and geographic footprint but year over year growth, total GP and current press releases)

3. FOLLOW UP

After each interview it is important to follow up with the interviewer expressing your appreciation for his or her time. If you are interested in the position, you must explain why you are a great fit for the job and ask for the job in your follow up email. A simple email such as:

Irene,

It was a pleasure to meet you today, thank you for your time and consideration regarding your training role in Calgary. I feel that my nine years training experience at INITECH coupled with my strong technical skills and personable nature make me an ideal fit for this role. I am very interest in pursuing next steps with CCI Ltd and look forward to your correspondence.

Kindest Regards,

John

A follow up email or letter should be sent within 24 hours of the interview. If you haven't heard from the recruiter within a week, send another follow up email or call.

If you are not interested in the position, it is still important to follow up with the recruiter. You never know what the future holds or who they know and one day you may need to reach out to this person again. A simple email stating the following will suffice:

Irene,

It was a pleasure to finally meet you today, thank you for your time and consideration regarding your training role in Calgary. Although the position sounds very interesting and I have a great deal of respect for CCI Ltd, I would like to withdraw my application. After giving our conversation careful consideration, I feel that this position isn't the right career move for me at this time. Again, thank you for your time.

Kindest Regards,
John

4. HOW MUCH ARE YOU WORTH?

Inevitably, at some point during the screening process, you are going to be asked the question - *How much money do you want*? Your answer should be based on what someone with your skills and education are worth in today's market. There are several great websites which provide this information free of charge. A site commonly used by our staff is *www.salary.com.* To find other sites, simple conduct Google ™, Yahoo ™ and bing™ searches using the following key words: *"Salary Finder "or "Salary Calculator"*.

You have just been tossed a hot potato. Don't get stuck holding it. You will get burned. Pass it back to them. The best way to deflect the question is to ask another question - *"According to industry standards someone with my years of experience living in Boston typically earns between $75K-$90K, what range were you thinking?"*

Never get stuck holding the hot potato!

5. OFFER NEGOTIATIONS

Before you begin offer negotiations with a potential employer, you must know what your bottom line is. Meaning if an employer offers you a compensation package below a certain value, you will walk away - no matter what. When considering your compensation package, don't focus solely on salary. Consider the employer's complete benefit package, your commute time to work, travel requirements of the job, number of vacation days, opportunity for advancement, job responsibilities etc.

When presented with an official offer, ask yourself if it is acceptable *"as is"*. If a company cannot meet your salary demands, there may be other things you can ask for to make up the difference, such as: an additional week of vacation, paid cell phone or car allowance, training and education, stock options etc.

If you are unhappy with the offer, the best time to discuss it with an employer is right away. Politely tell them that according to industry standards you were expecting more and provide them with a number and justify why you want more money. As an example:

The golden rule of negotiating is, "the person who talks first, always loses!" Have them give you a number first. There will be some awkward silence as you wait for them to answer.

"Margaret, I am flattered that you would offer me a position and I am very interested in working for ABV Ltd; however, I was anticipating the offer would be higher and more in line with industry standards. In my current role, I earn $80K per annum with no travel. As much as I would like to, I can't justify leaving my current job for a position that pays $75K and requires 40% travel. If you could increase the offer to $85K, I would accept it."

If they can't offer additional money ask, *how do they intend to assist you in meeting the difference?*

Whatever you leave on the negotiating table will stay on the negotiating table. Make sure you ask for everything up front, otherwise two years from now you will be referring to this book once again.

Most employers anticipate that candidates will counter-offer, and leave room for some negotiation.

6. HOW TO ACCEPT/DECLINE OFFERS

Hopefully, your job search story has a happy ending. If you are satisfied with the offer, wait 24 hours, read the fine print and accept it.

However, if you couldn't get what you were hoping for during your negotiations, never decline the offer on the spot. Always ask for 24 hours to think things over and sleep on it. Nothing brings clarity to a situation like a good night's sleep. If the following day, you are still unsatisfied with the job offer, then politely decline in writing. Don't wait for your start date to reject the offer.

Politeness is key for many reasons:

You don't know who the hiring manager knows or if you will apply to this company again.

Hiring managers change companies and typically you always run into the same people in your industry.

Although rare, sometimes companies do come back with a more lucrative compensation package.

TASKS:

1. Get your interview clothes ready. Polish your shoes and dry clean your suit.

When interviewing:

1. Do not forget to research the company you will be interviewing with. Prepare your list of questions for the individuals interviewing you.

2. Practice speaking to an unfamiliar audience. The easiest way, is to strike up a conversation with a complete stranger the next time you are standing in line at the grocery store.

Using the success map 122

PLAN THE FISHING TRIP

CHAPTER 07

You can have your tackle box loaded with all the best lures and your finest fishing pole packed but if you don't have a map to the fishing pond, you will squander precious time driving up and down the highway looking for the turnoff.

1. USING THE SUCCESS MAP

It is easy to lose focus and squander valuable time during your job search. To help you maximize your time and expedite your job search we have developed an easy to follow Success Map. Step-by-step, day-by-day the Success Map will keep you focused and guide you to your next great job.

Using your Success Map, **each evening you will plan for the following day's job search**. This exercise should only take about 15-20 minutes. For those *non-planners* this will be a challenging task; however,

BY FAILING TO PLAN, YOU PLAN TO FAIL!

In the subsequent pages we will show you how to use the *Success Map*.

It is available for download from our Resource Center at *www.uglyresumes.com*. You will require at least twenty copies to start. We suggest storing these sheets in a binder on your desk, electronically on a flash drive or a folder on your laptop.

THE SUCCESS MAP

Goal:				✓		Date:	
\multicolumn{8}{c}{TODAY'S INTERVIEWS}
TIME	LOCATION	COMPANY	INTERVIEWER & TITLE	TELEPHONE	EMAIL	POSITION	

LAND YOUR TROPHY FISH

	TODAY'S FOLLOW UP						
RE:	POSITION	COMPANY	CONTACT NAME & TITLE	TELEPHONE	EMAIL	\multicolumn{2}{c}{OUTCOME}
INTRW / APP						✓	MSG
INTRW / APP						✓	MSG
INTRW / APP						✓	MSG
INTRW / APP						✓	MSG
INTRW / APP						✓	MSG
INTRW / APP						✓	MSG
INTRW / APP						✓	MSG
INTRW / APP						✓	MSG
INTRW / APP						✓	MSG

FIND YOUR FISH

	NETWORK, NETWORK, NETWORK - FIND THE HIDDEN 80% OF JOBS!						
NETWORK	CONTACT NAME & TITLE	COMPANY	TELEPHONE	EMAIL	\multicolumn{2}{c}{OUTCOME}	LEAD?
PERSONAL					✓	MSG	Yes No
PROFESSIONAL					✓	MSG	Yes No
CO. OF INTEREST					✓	MSG	Yes No
CO. OF INTEREST					✓	MSG	Yes No
3RD PARTY RECRUITER					✓	MSG	Yes No

\multicolumn{7}{c}{SEARCH & APPLY TO THE ADVERTISED JOB MARKET}
SOURCE	POSITION	COMPANY	CONTACT NAME & TITLE	TELEPHONE	EMAIL	✓

This sample Success Map has been completed by a job seeker who is looking for an Operations Manager position. Note: the job seeker has planned for the following day's job search activities

Goal: Operations Manager				✓		Date: 7/5/2009	
TODAY'S INTERVIEWS							
	TIME	LOCATION	COMPANY	INTERVIEWER & TITLE	TELEPHONE	EMAIL	POSITION
	10:30	Telephone	Adel Inc	Frank Hall HR Director	712-555-9999	fh@strickland.com	Operation Mgr
TODAY'S FOLLOW UP							
	RE:	POSITION	COMPANY	CONTACT NAME & TITLE	TELEPHONE	EMAIL	OUTCOME
	INTRW / APP	Operation Mgr	Fennet Industries	Kyle Lovitt - President	712-555-1212	kyle@dennit.com	✓ MSG
	INTRW / APP	Operation Mgr	Entouch Ltd	Marg Peters - HR Manager	712-555-5659	marg.peters@et.com	✓ MSG
	INTRW / APP	Director of Ops	GYR Inc	Leslie Patel - Recruiting Mgr	712-555-4879	lp@gyr.com	✓ MSG
	INTRW / APP	Operation Mgr	Howard & Sons	Kevin Howard - Owner	712-555-3256	kevin@howard.com	✓ MSG
	INTRW / APP	Operation Mgr	YYZ Inc	Jack Smart - Director	712-555-6655	jsmart@yyz.com	✓ MSG
	INTRW / APP	General Mgr	Foxland Ltd	Bill Williams - HR Director	712-555-0001	wwilliams@foxland.com	✓ MSG
	INTRW / APP						✓ MSG
	INTRW / APP						✓ MSG
	INTRW / APP						✓ MSG
	INTRW / APP						✓ MSG

LAND YOUR TROPHY FISH

NETWORK, NETWORK, NETWORK - FIND THE HIDDEN 80% OF JOBS!						
NETWORK	CONTACT NAME & TITLE	COMPANY	TELEPHONE	EMAIL	OUTCOME	LEAD?
PERSONAL	Blake Johnson	Unemployed	712-555-3333	blake@freemail.com	✓ MSG	Yes No
PROFESSIONAL	Aneisha Patel - Ops Mgr	Jones & Thomson	712-555-6898	apatel@jt.com	✓ MSG	Yes No
CO. OF INTEREST	Hunderland Ltd				✓ MSG	Yes No
CO. OF INTEREST	Gates Technology Inc				✓ MSG	Yes No
3RD PARTY RECRUITER	Geniune Recruiters Ltd				✓ MSG	Yes No

SEARCH & APPLY TO THE ADVERTISED JOB MARKET					
SOURCE	POSITION	COMPANY	CONTACT NAME & TITLE	TELEPHONE	EMAIL	✓
www.monster.com						
ww.operationsjobs.co						
ATL Association						

FIND YOUR FISH

Let's deconstruct the different sections of the Success Map,

i] SECTION | HEADER

Goal: *To keep you focused on your job search goal, each day enter your desired job title (identified in Chapter One).*

✓ *Circle this as soon as the job offer has been signed!*

Date: *Enter the following day's date (Remember, you are planning for the next day)*

ii] SECTION | TODAY'S INTERVIEWS

TODAY'S INTERVIEWS						
TIME	LOCATION	COMPANY	INTERVIEWER & TITLE	TELEPHONE	EMAIL	POSITION
10:30	Telephone	Adel Inc	Frank Hall HR Director	712-555-9999	fh@strickland.com	Operation Mgr

This section is used to schedule interviews.

TIME *Enter the time of the interview. Confirm the time and be available 15 minutes early. If the interviewer is in a different part of the country or world, confirm the time zone as well.*

LOCATION *Enter the location of the interview. If the company has more than one local office, confirm the address. If it is a telephone or video interview, enter "phone" or "video".*

COMPANY *Enter the company name*

INTERVIEWER & TITLE *Enter the name and title of the person conducting the interview.*

Complete the remaining columns with the appropriate information.

iii]   Section | Todays folow up

As your job search progresses, you will find that this section is filled with more and more activities. Follow up activities should be scheduled immediately. For example, apply for a job, schedule a follow up call to the hiring manager in five days.

FOLLOW UP RULES

1) Follow up on interviews with a *thank-you* email within 24 hours.

2) Follow up on the status of interviews weekly.

3) Follow up on both online and offline applications five business days after you have submitted your resume.

4) If you leave a voice message or send an email to a hiring manager and they do not respond, wait three days and try again.

5) If after the second attempt the hiring manager doesn't respond, move on and focus your efforts on another position.

6) Follow up with key decision makers you have spoken with every month. A brief

Follow up is crucial to your job search. Don't wait till the end of the day to schedule all your follow-ups, you may forget an important call!

email stating that you are still seeking employment works best.

			TODAY'S FOLLOW UP			
RE:	POSITION	COMPANY	CONTACT NAME & TITLE	TELEPHONE	EMAIL	OUTCOME
INTRW / APP	Operation Mgr	Fennet Industries	Kyle Lovitt - President	712-555-1212	kyle@dennit.com	✓ MSG
INTRW / APP	Operation Mgr	Entouch Ltd	Marg Peters - HR Manager	712-555-5659	marg.peters@et.com	✓ MSG
INTRW / APP	Director of Ops	GYR Inc	Leslie Patel - Recruiting Mgr	712-555-4879	lp@gyr.com	✓ MSG
INTRW / APP	Operation Mgr	Howard & Sons	Kevin Howard - Owner	712-555-3256	kevin@howard.com	✓ MSG
INTRW / APP	Operation Mgr	YYZ Inc	Jack Smart - Director	712-555-6655	jsmart@yyz.com	✓ MSG
INTRW / APP	General Mgr	Foxland Ltd	Bill Williams - HR Director	712-555-0001	wwilliams@foxland.com	✓ MSG
INTRW / APP						✓ MSG
INTRW / APP						✓ MSG
INTRW / APP						✓ MSG
INTRW / APP						✓ MSG

In the **RE** column record whether the follow up pertains to an interview (INTRW) or application (APP). Interview follow ups take precedence over all other follow up.

In the **OUTCOME** column record whether or not you spoke with the person (check mark) or left a message (MSG). If this is your first message to this contact, schedule another call three days from now.

iv] Section | Network, Network, Network

Each day contact one person in your personal network and one person in your professional network. Actively market yourself to two companies and one recruiter who specializes in your industry.

During your planning session, fill in as much contact information as you have for the following day's calls/emails.

FIND YOUR	NETWORK, NETWORK, NETWORK - FIND THE HIDDEN 80% OF JOBS!				
	NETWORK	CONTACT NAME & TITLE	COMPANY	TELEPHONE	EMAIL
	PERSONAL	Blake Johnson	Unemployed	712-555-3333	blake@freemail.com
	PROFESSIONAL	Aneisha Patel - Ops Mgr	Jones & Thomson	712-555-6898	apatel@jt.com
	CO. OF INTEREST	Hunderland Ltd			
	CO. OF INTEREST	Gates Technology Inc			
	3RD PARTY RECRUITER	Geniune Recruiters Ltd			

If you speak to the contact the following day, circle the check mark in the OUTCOME column. If you leave a message, be sure to schedule a follow up call in three days.

OUTCOME		LEAD?	
✓	MSG	Yes	No
✓	MSG	Yes	No
✓	MSG	Yes	No
✓	MSG	Yes	No
✓	MSG	Yes	No

In the LEAD column, record whether or not the contact produced a job lead. *If someone is able to give you a job lead once, they may be able to provide another lead later on in your job search.*

v] SECTION | THE ADVERTISED JOB MARKET

During your planning session, choose three places you will look for advertised jobs. In the SOURCES column, enter the name of the job board, association, networking group, etc you plan to search. The following day, record all the pertinent information about the positions you have applied to. (*Remember to schedule a follow up in five days*).

SEARCH & APPLY TO THE ADVERTISED JOB MARKET						
SOURCE	POSITION	COMPANY	CONTACT NAME & TITLE	TELEPHONE	EMAIL	✓
www.monster.com						
www.operationsjobs.com						

Each day try to use a different combination of sources. You don't know where your next great job may be advertised.

Download your Success Map at www.uglyresumes.com.

CASE STUDY I – JACK WISEMAN   132

CASE STUDY II – SUSAN McMASTER   141

CASE STUDIES

APPENDIX aa

The quandary of the modern resume is that it must appeal to two different audiences, the software that stores and processes it and the human who decides to move forward with it. A successful resume will contain enough logic to satisfy the technology and enough knowledge to satisfy the human.

1. CASE STUDY I – JACK WISEMAN

Jack is a forty-one year old salesman with twelve years experience in the software industry. He has a successful track record in sales, but no formalized education past high school. He has excellent references from former co-workers and managers which support his strong sales ability. Unfortunately, Jack has spent his career working for unstable, medium sized technology companies. His most recent employer has filed bankruptcy and Jack has been tossed into the job market once again. Jack enjoys sales and technology and would like to stay in his field but would like to work for a large, international corporation.

Jack found the following position advertised in an industry trade magazine:

JOIN A LEADER IN THE GLOBAL SOFTWARE INDUSTRY! *Our client list includes some of the largest Fortune 500 manufacturers and the world's fastest growing emerging businesses. As part of our expansion into the North American market, we are actively seeking a dynamic, success-driven Account Manager to develop a new territory throughout the Carolinas, Georgia, Florida, and Tennessee. As part of the Software Services International team, the Account Manager will join a team of more than 15,000 employees. Our company offers a competitive benefit plan, stock options, paid vacation, and a generous compensation plan.*

Responsibilities:

Sell software and service offerings to businesses in the assigned territory
Develop pipeline of qualified leads
Cold call on prospective customers, including C-Level Executives
Collaborate with technical staff to develop customized product demonstrations
Evaluate and summarize monthly activity and forecasts
Maintain on-going relationships with accounts

Qualifications:

Minimum five (5) years technical sales experience
Must have a "hunter" type mentality
Track record of exceeding annual quotas
Ability to develop and nurture C-Level relationship
New territory development experience a must
Must be able to work with minimal supervision
Must be willing to travel 50-60% throughout territory
Prefer Bachelor's Degree

Applicants may email their resume to Donald@softwareservicesinternational.com.

Software Services International 45222 Ballantyne Drive, Charlotte, NC 28277
Tel: 704.333.3333 Fax: 704.444.4444 Web: www.softwareservicesinternational.com

---

Interested in this position, Jack **faxed** the following resume to Software Services International.

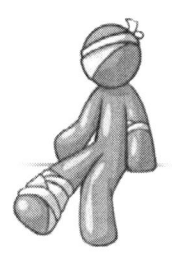

Unless the hiring company specifically requests a faxed resume, DO NOT fax your resume! In today's technology driven world, email and the online submissions of resumes are standard protocol. A faxed resume may imply a lack of basic technical skill required to do most jobs.

Jack Wiseman
3478 MAPLE DRIVE,
CHARLOTTE, NC 28277
HOME – 704-555-1111

OBJECTIVE: TO OBTAIN A SALES POSITION WHERE I CAN ADVANCE MY CAREER

EMPLOYMENT HISTORY

2007 – Pres   ULTIMATE CONSULTING, Charlotte, NC
Regional Engineering Software Representative

Sold engineering software to customers in North Carolina, South Carolina and Georgia

2006 – 2007   ENGINEER'S RESOURCE GROUP, Charlotte, NC
Account Manager

Sold engineering software to customers in North Carolina, South Carolina, Georgia and Florida

2005 – 2006   THE ZED GROUP, Charlotte, NC
Southern Rep

Sold engineering software to customers in North Carolina, South Carolina and Georgia

1996 – 2005   RED LIGHT ENGINEERING SOFTWARE INC, Raleigh, NC
Account Director

Sold engineering software throughout Florida

EDUCATION:

Pine Grove High School
Graduated 1985

ERRORS WITH JACK'S RESUME

Jack Wiseman
3478 MAPLE DRIVE,
CHARLOTTE, NC 28277
HOME – 704-555-1111

ERROR: No email address provided.

ERROR: No alternative day time phone number provided.

OBJECTIVE: TO OBTAIN A SALES POSITION WHERE I CAN ADVANCE MY CAREER

DO NOT include an objective. Objectives are about the needs of the candidate, not the needs of the employer. Your resume should be a synopsis of how you can help a company.

Remember, you want to make it easy for the hiring company to reach you.

APPENDIX aa | CASE STUDIES

ERROR: Dates of Employment – Provide specific start date (MM/YY) and end dates (MM/YY).

ERROR: The appearance of job hopping, companies are less likely to take a chance on a candidate who has had several positions in such a short period of time.

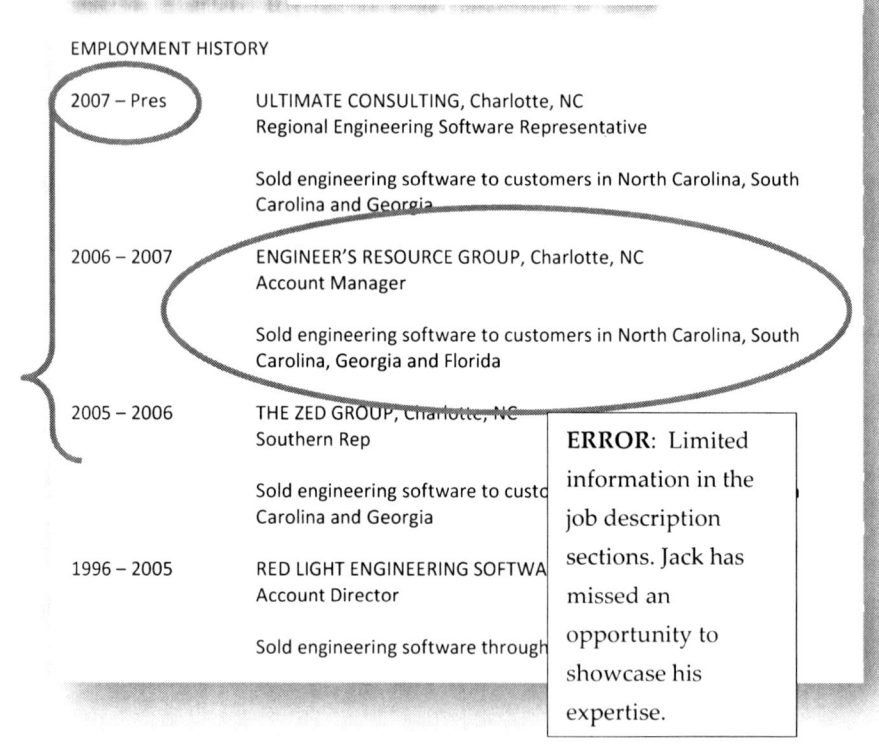

ERROR: Lack of industry keywords. Jack has reduced the odds that his resume will appear in database searches.

EMPLOYMENT HISTORY

2007 – Pres   ULTIMATE CONSULTING, Charlotte, NC
Regional Engineering Software Representative

Sold engineering software to customers in North Carolina, South Carolina and Georgia.

2006 – 2007   ENGINEER'S RESOURCE GROUP, Charlotte, NC
Account Manager

Sold engineering software to customers in North Carolina, South Carolina, Georgia and Florida

2005 – 2006   THE ZED GROUP, Charlotte, NC
Southern Rep

Sold engineering software to custo... Carolina and Georgia

1996 – 2005   RED LIGHT ENGINEERING SOFTWA...
Account Director

Sold engineering software through...

ERROR: Limited information in the job description sections. Jack has missed an opportunity to showcase his expertise.

Remember:

Paint a picture of a stellar employee by using action words and providing accurate information on your resume.

Recruiters will use keyword searches to find prospective candidates in the database, include as many industry key words as you can.

EDUCATION:

Pine Grove High School
Graduated 1985

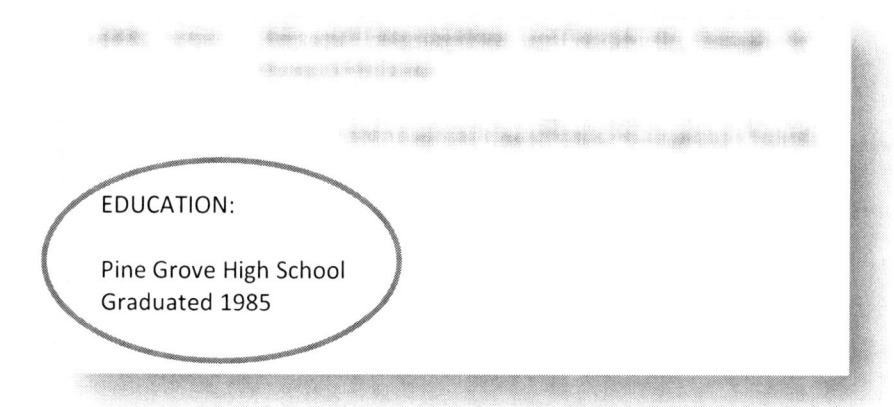

ERROR: DO NOT include your high school education on your resume. By including his high school education, Jack highlights the fact that he hasn't completed any post-secondary schooling.

JACK'S UGLY RESUME

Below we deconstruct Jack's new Ugly resume. He has saved the resume both as a WORD doc and a .txt (Plain Text) file.

If you are using Office 2007 remember to always save your resume in "Word 97-2003" format. If a company can't open your resume they'll never look at it!

JACK WISEMAN
3478 Maple Drive
Charlotte, NC 28277

Home: 704-555-1111 Cell: 704-555-2222
Email: Jack_wiseman@freemail.com

In this section, we added a cell number and an email address to make it easier for the hiring company to reach Jack.

By adding a profile, the Ugly Resume clearly explains why Jack is a fit for the position. As well we have omitted the objective.

PROFILE
Successful sales professional with more than 12 years experience selling software and technical services
Proven track record of exceeding annual quotas, winning business from competitors, and developing strong pipelines
Developed 2 new territories in the Southern United States, exceeded companies growth expectations
Hunter mentality with ability to cold call on C-level executives
Well versed in Software Services International line of product offerings

Remember, don't assume that the recruiter will be able to conclude you are the best candidate for the job, spell it out for them!

TECHNICAL SKILLS

Software Services International Products – Version 9.1 thru 11.5
Microsoft Office – Word, Excel, Power Point, Outlook

> *Although, Jack is not a technical guru in these products, he is able to use them and they should be included in his resume.*

ADDITIONAL TRAINING

2001	Selling to Business Executives	The North American Sales Institute
2002	How to Sell Services	The North American Sales Institute
2005	Prospecting – The Basics	The North American Sales Institute

Always list all the relevant training courses that are pertinent to the job you are applying for.

EMPLOYMENT HISTORY

01/08 – Pres   ULTIMATE CONSULTING, Charlotte, NC
www.ultimateconsulting.com
Actual Title: Regional Engineering Software Representative

We added "functional titles" to Jack's resume, making it more web searchable.

Functional Title: Sales, Account Manager, New Business Development, Technical Sales, Software Sales

- Currently sell software and services to businesses throughout North Carolina, South Carolina and Georgia
- Direct overall sales strategy and execution within the territory
- Develop marketing materials and customized presentations for key clients
- Grew territory from $0 to $2.3M in two quarters
- Secured over $1.5M in services business in the first quarter
- On track to close $7M in business by year end
- Surpassed 2008 quota of $1.8M

We added job descriptions that include action words and figures, now his job descriptions aren't simply a list of responsibilities, but rather paint a picture of successful employee.

Reason for Leaving: Company plans to close its North American Operations

03/06 – 12/07   ENGINEER'S RESOURCE GROUP, Charlotte, NC
www.engres.com
Actual Title: Account Manager

We added the company's web address to the resume, making it more searchable.

Functional Title: Sales, New Business Development, Technical Sales, Software Sales

- Sold Software International Products and services
- Developed key C-level relationships with manufacturers throughout North Carolina, South Carolina, Georgia and Florida
- Grew territory from $.5M to $6.5M in one year
- Exceeded first year quota by 110%
- Developed sales training program for new recruits
- Mentored two junior sales people
- Key note speaker at COE conference

Reason for Leaving: Company went bankrupt, closed operations.

We added "reason for leaving" although this line isn't required in most resumes we added it here to explain why Jack has had so many jobs in the past few years.

Download Jack's Ugly resume at www.uglyresumes.com

2. CASE STUDY II – SUSAN MCMASTER

Susan is a 35 year old Branch Manager at National Bank. She has completed her Bachelor's Degree in Finance and is currently pursuing her MBA. She has also completed several certifications. She is currently seeking a Branch Manager position that will offer her career advancement and better compensation.

Susan found the following job advertised on www.majorjobboard.com.

Big Bank Incorporated, the country's largest financial institution currently has an opening for a Branch Manager at one of its busiest branches in Metro Toronto. In this role, the Branch Manager will manage a team of 35-40 professionals in a fast-environment, as well as:

Lead the sales team to achieve new business acquisition goals
Ensure a superior level of customer service is achieved throughout the branch, and customer service goals are exceeded
Provide sales coaching to entire team
Act as a final point of contact for issue resolution

Job Requirements:
Three (3) years previous Branch Management experience at a major financial institution
Proven track record of meeting branch sales goals
Experience in both business and personal banking a must
Must be a licensed mutual fund salesperson
Strong relationship building skills
Strong people management skills
Bachelor's Degree

In response to the advertisement Susan emailed the following resume:

Although text boxes and shadowing may look great, they may prevent her resume from being properly downloaded into a company's applicant tracking system and or an online job board, making it nearly impossible for a recruiter to find her!

SUSAN MCMASTER 222 YONGE'S WAY, TORONTO, ON M5G 2B5
CELL: 416-888-9999 EMAIL: SUSAN.MCMASTER@NATIONALBANK.COM
Personal Website: www.sassysusan.com

HIGHLIGHT OF SKILLS

Holds University Degree

Pursuing MBA

Two years branch management experience

10 years banking experience

Excellent communication skills

Trilingual (English, French and Spanish)

EDUCATION

Bachelor of Commerce, U of T — UNIVERSITY OF TORONTO

MBA Queens — Queen's SCHOOL OF BUSINESS

ADDITIONAL CERTIFICATIONS

MUTUAL FUND LICENSE
AMP

EMPLOYMENT HISTORY

June 1998 – Pres   National Bank

Branch Manager

Responsible for managing a branch of 20 people
Responsible for sales goals and service goals
Handle customer services issues
Responsible for in branch promotions and customer appreciation days

Assistant Branch Manager

Responsible for assisting in the management of a branch staff of 10
Handled all staff scheduling
Responsible for commercial business development
Help resolve any problems in branch

Financial Services Representative

Responsible for assisting clients with mortgages and mutual funds
Cross sold products to customers
Provided excellent customer service to clients

ERRORS WITH SUSAN'S RESUME

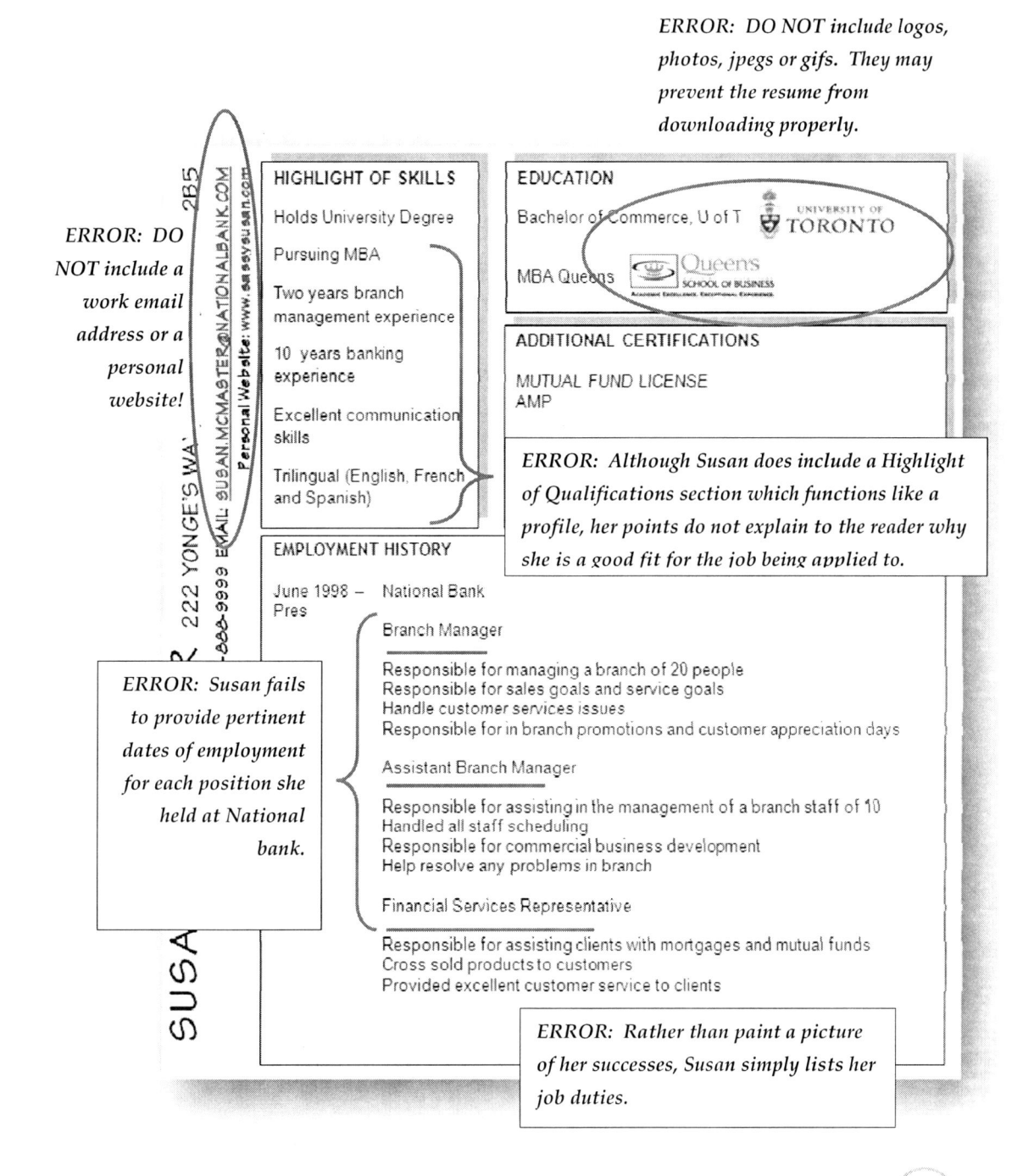

ERROR: DO NOT include logos, photos, jpegs or gifs. They may prevent the resume from downloading properly.

ERROR: DO NOT include a work email address or a personal website!

222 YONGE'S WAY 2B5 1-888-9999 EMAIL: SUSAN.MCMASTER@NATIONALBANK.COM Personal Website: www.sassysusan.com

SUSAN

HIGHLIGHT OF SKILLS
- Holds University Degree
- Pursuing MBA
- Two years branch management experience
- 10 years banking experience
- Excellent communication skills
- Trilingual (English, French and Spanish)

EDUCATION
Bachelor of Commerce, U of T   UNIVERSITY OF TORONTO

MBA Queens   Queen's SCHOOL OF BUSINESS

ADDITIONAL CERTIFICATIONS
MUTUAL FUND LICENSE
AMP

ERROR: Although Susan does include a Highlight of Qualifications section which functions like a profile, her points do not explain to the reader why she is a good fit for the job being applied to.

EMPLOYMENT HISTORY

June 1998 – Pres   National Bank

Branch Manager
- Responsible for managing a branch of 20 people
- Responsible for sales goals and service goals
- Handle customer services issues
- Responsible for in branch promotions and customer appreciation days

Assistant Branch Manager
- Responsible for assisting in the management of a branch staff of 10
- Handled all staff scheduling
- Responsible for commercial business development
- Help resolve any problems in branch

Financial Services Representative
- Responsible for assisting clients with mortgages and mutual funds
- Cross sold products to customers
- Provided excellent customer service to clients

ERROR: Susan fails to provide pertinent dates of employment for each position she held at National bank.

ERROR: Rather than paint a picture of her successes, Susan simply lists her job duties.

APPENDIX aa | CASE STUDIES   143

SUSAN'S UGLY RESUME

Below we deconstruct Susan's Ugly Resume that is now ready to be submitted to Big Bank Incorporated. She has saved the resume both as a "WORD 97-2003" doc and a .txt file (Plain Text).

Once you save your resume in a Plain Text format, remember to re-open and edit it as spacing and tabs are usually lost in the conversion.

SUSAN MCMASTER
222 Yonge's Way, Toronto, ON M5G 2B5
Cell: 416-888-9999 Email: susanm@freemail.com

In this section, we added a personal email address and omitted Susan's work email address.

Remember most employers have the ability to monitor your company email.

PROFILE

Degreed Branch Manager with nearly seven years experience at National Bank
Award winning track record of exceeding sales goals
Solid understanding of both personal and business banking
Holds mutual fund license
Excellent relationship builder, with a loyal client following
Successfully managed teams of up to 20 employees, earning Branch Manager of the Year Award
Excellent communications skills and a strong desire to succeed

In this section we changed Susan's Highlights of Skills to reflect the requirements of the job.

In this section we changed the order of Susan's Degrees.

EDUCATION

Currently Enrolled	Queen's University, Kingston, ON MBA
1997	University of Toronto, Toronto, ON Bachelor of Commerce

Put the most recent education first. We also included the location of each school as well. Although it isn't pertinent, we also added Susan's graduation date.

CERTIFICATIONS and LICENSES

2003 CSI
AMP- Accredited Mortgage Professional

In this section we added specific details about Susan's licenses and certifications because recruiters want to know how current certifications are.

June 1998 Pres	**National Bank, Toronto, ON** Branch Manager (September 2001 – Pres) Promoted to Branch Manager Provide guidance, including sales and service coaching to a staff of more than 20 people Act as a focal point for issue resolution within the branch Grew branch portfolio by 200% within two years through cold-calling, in branch promotions, and intensive sales mentoring program Won Customer Satisfaction Survey four years in a row for superior customer service levels Awarded Branch Manager of the Year Award for Superior Sales and Service 2007 Assistant Branch Manager (July 99 – September 2001) Promoted to Assistant Branch Manager Provided direction to 10 indirect reports, developed weekly schedule for branch staff, acted as the first line of defense for issue resolution Increased branch teller sales by 45% by providing mentoring to the front line staff Managed a portfolio of over 25M in commercial business Grew commercial portfolio by 25% within the first year Exceeded sales goals by more than 50% two years in a row Financial Services Representative (June 98 – July 99) Managed a portfolio of three hundred personal banking clients Increased retirement savings accounts by 30% Surpassed mutual funds deposit goals by 25% Exceeded mortgage goals by 75% Lured three real estate investment clients, with a total $8.5M in mortgage and investment business, away from a major competitor Won Excellence in Customer Service Award

> *In this section, we have taken Susan's list of responsibilities and changed them into a list of accomplishments that paint a picture of a successful candidate.*

> *We also provided specific details about her employment at National Bank including dates of employment for each position. This shows that she quickly moved through the ranks of the bank.*

YOUR PROFILE 149

YOUR PROFILE

APPENDIX ab

Third party recruiters and professional resume writing specialists know that the secret to getting a resume noticed is to create a candidate profile at the beginning of a resume. A profile highlights a candidate's accomplishments and explains why the candidate is the best person for the job.

In this Appendix, we will walk you through the process of creating an effective profile.

When submitting a general application to a company read through your resume and highlight your accomplishments and pertinent experience. In point form and using plenty of descriptive words list your accomplishments and experience under the Profile heading. Candidates will often highlight their education, years of experience, goals achieved and specific project successes in their profile.

When applying to a specific job, carefully read through the job description and match the job requirements to your experience, education and personality. If you can't find commonality between your experience and the requirements of the job then do not apply. Remember *Rules of the Search* - Don't set yourself up for failure by applying to jobs that you are either over-qualified or under-qualified for.

Let's look at an example. Read through the following job description posted by a third party recruiter on *www.majorjobboard.com* for a CFO (Chief Financial Officer).

If you are having problems highlighting your successes and pertinent experience, ask a friend to help you out.

> *CFO*
>
> *We have been retained by a leading window and door manufacturer to locate a CFO for their corporate office in Chicago, IL. Reporting directly to the CEO, the CFO will be responsible for the overall financial affairs of a $75 Million privately held family owned corporation. The CFO will direct the activities of the accounting office, including managing a team of 5 employees. He / she will also be responsible for preparing annual financial statements, annual budgets, and tax returns; implementing strict financial controls; supervising all cash flow within the organization; and working closely with external auditors.*
>
> *Qualified applicants must have:*
>
> *Three (3) – Five (5) years experience as a CFO in a similar sized company*
> *Previous manufacturing experience, prefer companies related to home building*
> *CPA or MBA*
> *The ability to work with a diverse group of individuals*
> *Ability for limited travel (Up to 20%) throughout the United States*
> *Strong team building skills, and must be meticulous and thorough*

STEP 1: Line per line, match your qualifications against the job requirements. If you do not have the exact requirement, but have similar experience it is worth putting it down (see second requirement). In this example, a qualified candidate would add the following:

A recruiter's expertise lies in his or her ability to find and evaluate candidates. Although many recruiters will have a good understanding of what your job entails and the technology you use, they are not experts in your field. Therefore, your profile must clearly state "why" you are the right person for the job.

Three (3) – Five (5) years experience as a CFO in a similar sized company

- *Eight (8) years experience as a CFO at a $100 million company*

Previous manufacturing experience, prefer companies related to home building

- *No manufacturing experience, but did work for a big box company that sold windows and doors to homebuilders*

CPA or MBA

- *MBA Graduate*

The ability to work with a diverse group of individuals

- *Have worked with multicultural teams at different global offices*

> **Ability for limited travel (Up to 20%) throughout the United States**

- *Available for up to 50% travel*

> **Strong team building skills, and must be meticulous and thorough**

- *References will support this*

STEP 2: Match additional information found in the job description to your experience. If the job description doesn't include additional information then visit the company's website to find out details about the company, their industry, etc. In this example, a qualified candidate would add the following information:

> **privately held family owned corporation.**

- *Two (2) years experience working for a privately held family owned business*

Including previous accomplishments in your profile will help your resume stand out!

STEP 3: Highlight other key accomplishments found in your resume. In our example, the qualified applicant would add the following:

- *Helped an employer get out of bankruptcy*

- *Recognized as an up and coming business leader by the Chamber of Commerce*

STEP 4: Add descriptive, action words and phrases to your qualifications that will help the reader visualize a successful candidate. The qualified applicant in our example would add the following descriptive words and phrases,

Eight (8) years experience as a CFO at a $100 Million company becomes:

- **Highly regarded CFO with more than eight (8) years experience working for a thriving $100 million corporation**

No manufacturing experience, but did work for a big box company that sold windows and doors to homebuilders becomes:

- **Successfully managed the financial office of Builder's Expo, the leading retailer of windows and doors in the**

Midwest, operating within budget eight (8) consecutive years

CPA or MBA becomes:

- MBA graduate who possesses in-depth knowledge of corporate taxation laws and international accounting practices and procedures

The ability to work with a diverse group of individuals becomes:

- Effectively managed a diverse, global team of financial professionals located throughout North America, Europe and Asia

Available for up to 50% travel becomes:

- Willingness to go the extra mile, travel up to 50% acceptable

References will support this becomes:

- Successful record of building profitable teams that have led companies out of bankruptcy, developed balanced budgets and saved companies millions

- Well respected for meticulous and thorough nature

Two (2) years experience working for a privately held family owned business becomes:

- Solid understanding of the dynamics of a family owned business

Recognized as an up and coming business leader by the Chamber of Commerce becomes:

- Won the Prestigious Up and Coming Business Leader Award from the Chamber of Commerce

STEP 5: Rearrange the qualifications in importance. The qualified applicant would list his/her qualifications as such:

- Highly regarded CFO with more than eight (8) years experience working for a thriving $100 Million Corporation

- Successfully managed the Financial Office of Builder's Expo, the leading retailer of windows and doors in the Midwest, operating within budget eight (8) consecutive years

- Effectively managed a diverse, global team of financial professionals located throughout North America, Europe and Asia

- MBA graduate who possesses in-depth knowledge of corporate taxation laws and international accounting practices and procedures

- Willingness to go the extra mile, travel up to 50% acceptable

- Successful record of building profitable teams that have led companies out of bankruptcy, developed balanced budgets and saved companies millions

- Well respected for meticulous and thorough nature

- Solid understanding of the dynamics of a family owned business

- Won the Prestigious Up and Coming Business Leader Award from the Chamber of Commerce

KEYWORDS 159

KEYWORDS

APPENDIX ac

Remember: you want to paint a picture of a successful applicant who will have a positive impact on a potential employer. The following descriptive words may be used in your resume or email correspondence with potential employers.

Caution: Ensure that you know the meaning of all the words included in your resume! The misuse of a word could lead to the immediate rejection of your application.

Accelerated, Achieved, Adapted, Addressed, Administered, Analyzed, Approved, Assembled, Able, Achiever, Active, Adaptable, Adept, Ambitious, Analytical, Assertive, Astute, Attentive

Balanced, Built, Bright, Boundless, Broad-minded

Communicated, Completed, Computed, Comprehensive, Conceived, Consolidated, Constructed, Contracted, Contributed, Coordinated, Created, Capable, Challenge-oriented, Competent, Conscientious, Considerate, Cooperative, Courteous, Creative

Defined, Delegated, Developed, Devised, Directed, Dedicated, Dependable, Determined, Devoted, Disciplined, Dynamic

Edited, Enlisted, Established, Evaluated, Examined, Executed, Expanded, Experienced, Effective, Efficient, Energetic, Enterprising

The easiest way to validate the meaning of a word is to use the WORD Thesaurus. Click on the word you want to use, hold the shift key and press the F7 key.

Fabricated, Facilitate, Formulate, Fostered, Fulfilled, Faithful, Far-reaching, Fast Learner, Fearless, Firm

Generated, Granted, Guided, Go-getter

Helpful

Implemented, Improved, Incorporated, Increased, Initiated, Inspired, Instructed Interpreted, Investigated, Imaginative, Impressive, Independent, Industrious, Innovative, Insightful, Inventive

Judicious

Launched, Led, Lectured, Large-scale, Listen carefully, Logical

Maintained, Managed, Mastered, Mediated, Moderated, Motivated, Methodical,

Operated, Organized, Originated, Outlined, Overhauled, Oversaw, Optimistic, Of good judgment, Orderly, Organized

Participated, Performed, Persuaded, Pinpointed, Planned, Prepared, Presented, Prioritized Programmed, Promoted, Proposed, Proved, Perceptive, Personable, Perspicacious, Pleasant,

Poised, Positive, Practical, Productive, Proficient, Problem Solver, Progressive, Prolific, Punctual

Recommended, Reduced, Reevaluated, Rejected, Reinforced, Renegotiated, Repaired, Repeated, Reported, Revamped, Reviewed, Revised

Realistic, Reliable, Resourceful, Responsible, Risk-taker

Scheduled, Sensible, Set-up, Simplified, Spoke, Solved, Streamlined, Strengthened, Structured Supervised, Supported, Surveyed, Self-reliant, Self-starter, Shrewd, Sincere, Skilled, Smart, Strong-Minded, Successful, Systematic

Taught, Trained, Translated, Tactful, Talented, Team Player, Thorough, Trustworthy

Updated, United, Unwavering

Worked, Wrote

Well thought out, Willing worker, Work well under pressure, Work well with others

JOB BOARDS

JOB BOARDS

APPENDIX ad

Throughout the book we show you how to fish for many of the top job sites on the web and even mention them by name. To further simply your search we have included WEDDLE's 2009 User's Choice Awards of top job websites, Canada's most popular Job Sites and how to identify the Niche Job Boards.

i] WEDDLE's 2009 User's Choice Awards

healthjobsusa.com	Indeed.com
AllHealthcareJobs.com	Job.com
AllRetailJobs.com	JobCircle.com
CareerBuilder.com	JobFox.com
Craigslist.org	Jobing™.com
Dice.com	TheLadders.com
DirectEmployers.com	Monster.com
DiversityJobs.com	Net-Temps.com
EmploymentGuide.com	SimplyHired.com
ExecuNet.com	6FigureJobs.com
GetTheJob.com	SnagAJob.com
GOJobs.com	TopUSAJobs.com
Hcareers.com	Vault.com
HealthCareerWeb.com	VetJobs.com
HEALTHeCAREERS.com	hotjobs.Yahoo.com

ii] MOST POPULAR CANADIAN JOB SITES

www.JobBank.gc.ca	www.Indeed.ca
www.Eluta.ca	www.Workopolis.ca
www.WowJobs.ca	www.JobBus.com
www.CareerBuilder.ca	www.Monster.ca
ca.Hotjobs.Yahoo.com	www.JobPostCanada.com
www.jobboom.com	www.kijiji.ca
www.careerbeacon.com	www.careerjet.ca

iii] NICHE JOB BOARDS

For a comprehensive list of niche job boards, visit the following:

www.internetinc.com. This site lists the top 100 niche job boards for 2008. Search the site for "top 100"

www.employmentwebsites.org. *The International Association of Employment Web Sites* allows you to browse both by industry and geography.

About the Authors

Jennifer Rallis is the CEO and Co-Founder of CORPX, a direct placement, technical recruiting firm. With nearly ten years recruiting experience for various sectors including: hospitality, banking, engineering and telecom; she has accrued an impressive list of customers from technology start-ups to Fortune 500 organizations. As an Alumnus of the University of Guelph, Jennifer began a notable career in banking then pursued her true passion, recruiting, where she has helped thousands of professionals advance their careers. In Ugly Resumes Get Jobs, Jennifer shares the inside secrets of the recruiting world with candidates who want to gain the competitive advantage in the race to their next great job.

Theo Rallis is a Process Consultant and Co-Founder of BM Imports. Armed with two degrees from Laurentian University and New Brunswick College and the motto "work smarter, not harder", Theo has spent more than a decade assisting Fortune 500 Manufacturers and SMBs adopt and leverage new engineering, design, manufacturing and information management software. For the past four years he has created and closed large solution opportunities by process mapping new technologies to client business initiatives. In Ugly Resumes Get Jobs, Theo applies the same principals and processes used by large corporations to achieve efficiency to the job search process. Not only has Theo developed the system, he has successfully used it to uncover several rewarding career opportunities.

Printed in the United States
221670BV00003B/1/P